Improving Schools and Inspection:
The self-inspecting school

Improving Schools and Inspection
The self-inspecting school

Neil Ferguson, Peter Earley, Brian Fidler and Janet Ouston

P·C·P

Paul Chapman
Publishing Ltd

Paul Chapman Publishing Ltd
A SAGE Publications Company
6 Bonhill Street
London EC2A 4PU

SAGE Publications Inc
2455 Teller Road
Thousand Oaks, California 91320

SAGE Publications India Pvt Ltd
32, M-Block Market
Greater Kailash -I
New Delhi 110 048

British Library Cataloguing in Publication data

A catalogue record for this book is available from the British Library

ISBN 0-7619-6726-5
ISBN 0-7619-6727-3 (pbk)

Library of Congress catalog card number available

Typeset by Dorwyn Ltd, Rowlands Castle, Hants
Printed and bound by Athenaeum Press, Tyne & Wear

Contents

Notes on Contributors

Neil Ferguson has worked in universities in England and Scotland. Formerly a head of a university School of Education, he has most recently been the research officer attached to the Nuffield Foundation funded project on school inspection based at the Institute.

Peter Earley is a senior lecturer in the Management Development Centre at the Institute of Education, University of London. He is course leader for the MA in Education Mangement and has recently directed two research projects on school inspection and school governors. He has published widely and his most recent book (with Michael Creese) is entitled *Improving Schools and Governing Bodies* (Routledge, 1999). He co-edits the practitioner journal *Professional Development Today*.

Brian Fidler is Professor of Education Management at the University of Reading. He is course leader for the MSc in Managing School Improvement and has published widely on aspects of school management, particularly strategy and staff appraisal. He is editor of the international journal *School Leadership and Management*.

Janet Ouston is a visiting fellow at the Institute of Education where she was head of the Management Development Centre until 1998. She is particularly interested in management theory which moves beyond the assumptions of rationality and has recently contributed to edited collections with articles entitled *Managing in Turbulent Times* and *School effectiveness and improvement: Critique of a movement*.

List of figures and tables

Abbreviations

CDC	Comparative data collection
DfE	Department for Education
DfEE	Department for Education and Employment
FSM	Free school meals
GCSE	General Certificate of Secondary Education
GM	Grant Maintained
HMCI	Her Majesty's Chief Inspector
HMI	Her Majesty's Inspectors (of Schools)
ICT	Information and Communication Technology
IEP	Independent Education Plan
INSET	In-service education and training
KIs	Key issues for action
KS	Key Stage
LEA	Local Education Authority
NFER	National Foundation for Educational Research
OfSTED	Office for Standards in Education
OFSTIN	Office for Standards in Inspection
PANDAs	Performance and Assessment Reports
PICSI	Pre-inspection context and school indicator
QCA	Qualifications and Curriculum Authority
RgI	Registered inspector
SATs	Standard Assessment Tasks
SDP	School Development Plan
SEN	Special Educational Needs
SIP	School Improvement Plan
SMT	School Management Team
TES	*Times Educational Supplement*

Acknowledgements

We would like to express our sincere thanks to the many people who made this research possible. Firstly to the schools, particularly the case study schools, and the registered inspectors who were good enough to give of their time to complete questionnaires, be interviewed and generally provide us with information about the experiences of inspection. Thanks must also go to OfSTED itself who have always been most helpful to the project and provided the research team with lists of schools and registered inspectors as well as giving up their own time to be interviewed or to respond to our enquiries. Jackie Davis, the research officer on the secondary schools project, is also warmly thanked for her contribution to the research, as is Michael Creese who provided helpful comments on the manuscript.

Lastly we are most grateful to the sponsors of our research, BEMAS, for their support for our initial postal surveys, and more recently, the Nuffield Foundation. In particular we wish to thank Dr Helen Quigley, the Nuffield Foundation's Head of Education, for her support over the last three years. Without the Nuffield Foundation's funding, this research would probably not have been successfully completed.

Foreword

I have seven pairs of reading glasses that I leave lying around in my home, office and car. They were bought in chemists and supermarkets and were selected using the eye charts that these shops provide and with a process that might be loosely described as 'self-inspection'. I have been to an optician for an eye test and felt uncomfortable when I was asked to show him the pair of spectacles that I had with me. He refused to recognise my glasses as glasses and would only refer to them as 'magnifiers'. He even asked me where I had 'found' them and in an act of extraordinary bravery I named the chain of chemists in which they had been bought.

The incident encapsulates the sales technique that is at the heart of professionalism. It depends on making the client feel dependent on services that must be provided in the approved way by a suitably qualified and accredited individual. It is an exercise in authority, validated by superior technical skill, that places the professional at an advantage. But spectacles have been 'demystified' by the anonymous army of technicians in the workshops of large specialist retailers and by the low-cost glasses sold in supermarkets and high street chemists. This endangers the livelihood of my optician, threatens his professional status and undermines his ability to establish exclusive rights to an area of expertise. He is in the process of being 'de-professionalised' which, in the definition provided by Jeffrey and Woods (1998, p.114), includes the 'weakening of control and autonomy, and in general, a move from professional to technician status'. My rights as a consumer and competition from the market-place have contributed to the diminution of my optician's professional status. I will ignore his warnings, reject his advice and refuse to pay a higher price for his services.

However, it is the enjoyment of professional power, the freedom to exercise professional judgement and pride in the application of highly developed skills that the professional finds rewarding. It may explain why professional careers attract high quality recruits and why confident professionals strive for high standards. The 'de-professionalisation' of an occupational group carries risks and bright young men and women of the next generation might want to think very carefully before deciding to follow my optician's chosen career path.

An OfSTED inspection places schools under scrutiny and heads, teachers and governors can no longer argue that they have the right to be the sole arbiters of their own standards. Families have the right to know whether their child's school is a challenging institution with a positive atmosphere or whether it has developed a negative climate in which teachers have become dispirited. It is also important to recognise the rights of the nation to information about its schools and the rights of the community to be assured that its local schools are effective institutions. There are risks in handing over the control of education to the professionals without asking who will protect the interests of pupils and their families and ensure that school staff do not become cynical or complacent.

In the recent past, governments in this country have felt the need to control professionals in education and restore the rights of the consumer by increasing state control through the creation of what has come to be called 'the audit society' (Power, 1997). In the 1980s when, for example, the London Borough of Croydon became an important political battleground, the *Times Educational Supplement* included such headlines as 'Boycott threat over tests which expose bad teachers' (*TES*, 9th December 1983). Donald Naismith, the borough's outspoken Director of Education, claimed, in an interview with the *TES*, that what is taught in schools is 'a bloody mystery' and went on to say that teachers were 'involved in fraud on a monumental scale'. More recently, MacBeath (1999, p. 5) has commented: 'When someone wants to defend something or to attack something, he (*sic*) often evaluates it' and quoting House (1973) concludes, 'Evaluation is an integral part of the political processes of our society'.

It is not always easy to realise that a political battle has been won, to decide when the moment for new initiatives has arrived or to recognise that the solution to one problem has created new difficulties that must be addressed. It is also important to remain vigilant, to seek out ways of developing the inspection process, to think constantly about the strategies that bring about improvements in schools and to consider the approach to inspection that might be in place before a second or third round of reinspections is begun. We argue that while it is important to preserve the benefits of inspection and ensure its continued progress, it is also important to take account of its shortcomings and consider how its unintended ill-effects might be ameliorated. As this book will argue, an approach to school improvement that was developed in reaction to the concerns of the 1980s may need to adapt to the changed climate of opinion which OfSTED itself has been instrumental in creating.

Neil Ferguson
October, 1999

1

Inspection and self-inspection

Previous generations of school teachers believed that they should be left alone to get on with the business of teaching behind the closed doors of their classrooms. Geer, for example, in a discussion about the attractions of teaching which was first published in the late 1960s, noted that there was still 'something of the lonely eminence of the classroom' and suggested that one of the advantages of membership of the teaching profession was that: 'visibility of performance is low and few people believe we have learned as yet how to measure teaching ability' (1968, p.7). It is difficult to see how a system that allowed so much personal and professional autonomy could combat inertia, encourage improvements or provide any guarantee that teachers would have appropriately high expectations of their pupils. However, that is a modern thought and one which is undoubtedly much influenced by the culture which has spawned the National Curriculum and its testing programme, the league tables of schools and, perhaps most significantly of all, the Office for Standards in Education (OfSTED) which has completed the external inspection of every state-controlled school in England and Wales[1] and, at the time of writing, is immersed in the first round of reinspections and about to introduce differentiated or 'light touch' inspections for a minority of schools.

The foreword to this book noted that the tradition of *laissez-faire* and dependence on teachers' professional judgements in educational matters had survived into the 1980s and had become a contentious issue. It might be argued that the introduction of any reasonably rigorous system of review and evaluation which was designed to change teachers' 'lonely eminence' and make schools more accountable was bound to have beneficial results. The main purpose of this book is to consider the system of OfSTED inspections and ask how beneficial it has been in encouraging schools to develop and improve. Has external inspection gone too far or not far enough? What are its advantages and disadvantages and are there alternative approaches to school assessment and improvement that might prove to

1

be more effective? There might, for example, be benefits in the introduction of systems of school self-evaluation or drawbacks which are so significant that it would be best to continue the current arrangements. The system of external inspections that the Office for Standards in Education has introduced for schools is still being developed in the light of the experience of the first round of inspections, but is it time to ask whether a third round of inspections should follow the same pattern or begin to move in new directions? This book draws upon our research findings and discusses what we have learned about the current system and its operation. It concludes by making suggestions about the possible future development of school inspection in England and Wales.

OfSTED inspection

The Office for Standards in Education, headed by Her Majesty's Chief Inspector (HMCI), was created as an independent, non-ministerial government department in September 1992. It was charged with the task of setting up a new system of school inspection and maintaining a sufficient number of qualified inspectors to fulfil the requirements of each inspection cycle. The Education (Schools) Act 1992 introduced a system of competitive bidding in which contracts for inspections could be awarded to registered inspectors or their employers. There are currently a large number of 'contractors' which are private businesses that recruit OfSTED-trained staff and compete for inspection contracts from the schedule of inspections which OfSTED has determined. This arrangement for the inspection of schools is very different from the arrangements for the inspection of other public services, such as prisons, probation and the social services (Mordaunt, 1999). Her Majesty's Inspectorate (HMI), the professional arm of OfSTED, inspects independent schools, teacher training institutions, and groups outside the school system, but has a major responsibility for the quality assurance of inspection teams and their contractors. It also has a significant role to play in relation to schools that are failing to provide an adequate standard of education for their pupils and are said to have 'serious weaknesses' or to be in need of 'special measures' (OfSTED, 1999a).

Every inspection is led by a registered inspector (RgI) who is usually called 'the lead inspector' because RgIs also join inspection teams that they do not lead. Although all RgIs and team inspectors (with the exception of the lay inspectors) are qualified teachers, there is no requirement for them to have any recent experience in schools and inspectors may be retired teachers or teacher trainers or local education authority (LEA) advisers. The initial qualification for a team inspector is a taught course of about five days spread over a three-month period. There is also a requirement to study five preparatory units, plus around a dozen distance learning units, and to complete assignments which are assessed by the course tutor. Most trainee inspectors would require a period of two or three months to complete all of these requirements and prepare for the final examinations. Registered inspectors must first gain experience as a team inspector and then successfully complete an additional programme of training.

The 1992 Education Act which set out the changes to the inspection system made it compulsory for every inspection team to include a 'lay' inspector who is someone 'without personal experience in the management of any school or the provision of education in any school'. Lay inspectors may now become registered inspectors and a small number have qualified as RgIs and take responsibility for leading inspection teams and writing the schools' inspection reports. The notion of a category of inspector who (initially at least) has little knowledge of the processes that he or she is employed to observe, might seem odd to those who are not familiar with the recent history of education in England. Lay inspectors were probably created as a symbolic representation of the public interest and as a reminder from government to teachers and inspectors that they should not claim exclusive rights to the ownership of the education process. The fact that it is the school's governing body – another group of lay individuals – and not the management team that is responsible for the school's response to the inspection report also helps to underline this message.

The logic of inspection

The 'Framework for Inspection' established the criteria on which schools were to be judged and set out a code of practice governing the conduct of inspections. These criteria, unlike those of the HMI system which OfSTED inspections replaced, are defined in detail and published (together with information about how they will be assessed) in a series of inspection handbooks (OfSTED, 1994/5) that are available to anyone who wishes to purchase them. All the new requirements which had been introduced since the publication of the handbooks were summarised in August 1997 in booklet form and distributed to all inspectors (OfSTED, 1997a). A briefing containing some guidance on their implementation was sent to schools some months later (OfSTED, 1998d). This policy of 'openness' is characteristic of the OfSTED system and enables schools to take account of the inspection criteria, particularly in school development planning. The first round of inspections was completed for all schools in 1998 and there is now a general acceptance that a school that does well in an inspection is, by definition, a 'good school' and schools with good reports are keen to publicise this in their prospectus and increasingly in advertisements for new members of staff. Before the introduction of OfSTED inspections, a 'good school' was more likely to be one with a good reputation among parents and the local community but the reasons why the school had won this trust and support were not always clear.

The inspection of schools under the new OfSTED Framework began in September 1993 in secondary schools (inspections in primary schools and special schools began a year later) and arrangements were made for every school to be inspected on a four-year cycle. Since the first inspections were carried out, the Framework has been revised and updated and there have been a number of changes introduced. (The main ones are summarised in Table 1.1.) However, although there have been changes in inspection policy and practice, the cornerstones of the process – judgements about the quality of education provided by the school, the educational standards achieved by pupils, the efficiency with which financial and other resources are managed and the spiritual, moral, social and cultural development of pupils – have remained the same.

Table 1.1   OfSTED inspection since 1992

Education Act 1992	OfSTED inspection established on a four-year cycle
Autumn term 1993	The first secondary schools inspected
Autumn term 1994	The first primary and special schools inspected
April 1996	The first major revision of the inspection criteria
December 1996	The Secretary of State announced that OfSTED was moving to a six-year cycle for some schools, and a shorter period for others
March 1997	OfSTED announced that 650 secondary schools would be reinspected in the academic year 1997/8. These were schools that had been inspected in the first two years of inspection, between September 1993 and July 1995
September 1997	Reinspection of secondary schools started
September 1998	Reinspection of primary and special schools started
November 1998	Consultation Paper *Proposals for a Differentiated System of School Inspections* published
March 1999	Revised system announced to include differentiated or 'light touch' inspections for some schools
January 2000	Revised framework introduced and new inspection system commences

Changes to the inspection system have tracked the changes in schools as heads, governors and staff have reacted to a series of government interventions and Acts of Parliament designed to raise educational standards and make schools more accountable to parents and the community. These changes (e.g. a focus on literacy and numeracy, an increased emphasis on information and communications technology, the increasing importance of monitoring, target-setting and the school's record of improvement, an emphasis on assessment) have had a considerable effect on the content of inspections. However, inspection is also a mechanism for delivering changes and ensuring that heads, governors and LEAs comply with new statutory requirements. As such, it reflects the values in which successive governments have placed their faith. Although school inspection is said to be 'independent', it is perhaps more appropriate, on occasions, to note its role as an arm of the state which has been created to ensure compliance.

The search for high standards through a market mechanism and competitive tendering is an important feature of the new inspection system and the publicity that attends a critical inspection report supposedly helps to empower the consumer as a force for change. So powerful are these forces for centrally induced changes that they cannot be ignored and the prospect of an impending inspection is sufficient to make teachers and heads feel apprehensive. The events of the period leading up to an inspection, the inspection week itself and the aftermath of inspection and the variety of evidence that inspectors collect during an inspection are briefly described in the next chapter. Teachers' reactions to inspection and their effect on school development are discussed in some detail in Chapters 3, 4, 5 and 6.

This book is about the process of external inspection and its influence on school development and improvement, but it is also about 'self-inspection'. The latter is a concept that requires some further discussion and definition because there are senses in which (i) all schools, (ii) few schools and (iii) no schools at all in England and Wales are 'self-inspecting' institutions.

Self-inspection

The Office for Standards in Education has had such a potent influence in schools in England and Wales that some commentators have become concerned about its power to dominate teachers' thinking and take charge of the education agenda. Cullingford (p. 59, 1999), for example, notes the emphasis that government places on the control of schools and suggests that 'the most significant demonstration of the belief in measures of external control is the power invested in OfSTED'. However, it is not simply the mechanisms of inspection that cause concern but the fact that the discussion of education that takes place in schools and elsewhere increasingly employs a vocabulary and transmits values that are dominated by the 'OfSTED discourse'. There is a new set of assumptions and a vocabulary to go with them. Few teachers now question that 'teaching quality', 'improvement since the last inspection', 'value for money', 'pupil progress in lessons', and 'the identification of weaknesses and serious weaknesses' can be assessed without undue difficulty, but these are big assumptions. It is too easy to overlook the fact that the judgements in inspection reports are *judgements* and that inferences made on the basis of classroom observations, the scrutiny of documents and pupils' work, and discussions with school staff and governors (see Chapter 2) are capable of a variety of interpretations that depend on the frame of reference and previous experience of the individual inspector.

Teachers' thinking is said to have been 'colonised' (Jeffrey and Woods, 1998; Lowe, 1998) by the OfSTED discourse and the way that teachers think about their work and evaluate their strengths and weaknesses is likely to have been influenced to a considerable extent by the Inspection Framework. The creation of an orthodoxy, and its power to influence the ways that schools judge themselves in the period between inspections, explains the sense in which all schools, or nearly all schools, might be said to be 'self-inspecting'. OfSTED's belief that no 'orthodoxy' exists has been supported by the Parliamentary Select Committee report on the work of OfSTED (House of Commons, 1999a) which declared:

> We agree with those witnesses who told us that, at present, there is little danger that schools will use the Inspection Framework in such a way that it has become an 'orthodoxy'. But the DfEE should not be complacent. We recommend that the DfEE keeps under review the ways in which schools use the Inspection Framework (paragraph 27).

OfSTED has also developed the systematic use of the Framework criteria for 'self-evaluation'. The publication *School Evaluation Matters* (OfSTED, 1998a) points out that:

> It is advantageous to base school self-evaluation on the same criteria as those used in all schools by inspectors. A common language has developed about the work of schools, expressed through the criteria. Teachers and governors know that the criteria reflect things that matter (paragraph 18).

This process of 'self-evaluation', it is suggested, should be conducted annually in the years between inspections and, when the time for an inspection arrives, the visiting inspectors can be expected to comment on its effectiveness in the inspection report. School self-evaluation, using the OfSTED criteria, is a form of 'self-inspection' and this description should, we believe, be used to distinguish the process from a variety of other self-evaluation methods that do not use the Framework criteria. This distinction is further developed in Chapter 11 which discusses the potential of both self-evaluation and 'self-inspection' as catalysts for school improvement.

To date, few schools have been involved in 'self-inspection' in the sense of a systematic application of the inspection criteria that is described in *School Evaluation Matters* (OfSTED, 1998a). This is set to change because OfSTED has developed new materials, more detailed guidance and training courses for senior school managers to be run by OfSTED-accredited trainers throughout England and Wales.

One of the arguments which this book will critically examine is the suggestion that self-evaluation using the OfSTED criteria (which we have called 'self-inspection') could become an integral part of the OfSTED inspection process. This would mean that schools would be involved in their own inspection, in a more significant way than at present, and that the results of 'self-inspection' would contribute to the outcomes of inspection. This might ensure that 'self-inspection' was not an optional extra and that the vast majority of schools, and not just those with a ready-made enthusiasm for self-evaluation, would be involved in a systematic 'self-inspection' process using the OfSTED criteria.

There might be important advantages gained from the development of a nation-wide system of this kind. There are also potential pitfalls which include worries about the perpetuation of the 'OfSTED orthodoxy', the effects of 'self-inspection' on staff relationships, and concerns about 'audit overkill' and the additional burden that some schools would find intolerable if self-inspection became a new requirement. 'Self-inspection' as an important element of the inspection process would not, as this book shows, be likely to be welcomed by OfSTED itself. There is currently no system within the United Kingdom which brings together external inspection and school 'self-inspection' and no immediate prospect that this might happen. It is in this sense that no school is a 'self-inspecting' school. However, it is important to explore the reasons why OfSTED is reluctant to allow schools to be involved in their own inspection and to decide whether it is a stance that should be supported or criticised.

Much of the evidence that has been brought to bear on such questions has been gathered in a series of Nuffield Foundation funded research projects into the impact of OfSTED inspection in primary and secondary schools. These projects, located at the Institute of Education, University of London since 1993, have been the subject of several research reports (Ouston, Fidler and Earley, 1998; Ouston *et al.*, 1998; Ferguson *et al.*, 1999a) and a summary of their main data sources is contained in the Appendix. However, it is not the purpose of this book to report the detailed findings of these projects. It aims to use the outcomes of the research to shed light on the questions that emerged from investigations into the various phases of the inspection process as they were experienced in schools.

The next chapter briefly chronicles some aspects of OfSTED's achievements, describes its approach, notes the characteristics of inspection's various phases and begins to comment on schools' characteristic reactions to their inspection teams. These are matters that are also discussed in later chapters. The purpose of Chapter 2 is to discuss aspects of the inspection process in order to clarify the particular perspective from which this book is written.

Chapter 3 looks at the pre-inspection period and heads' and teachers' reactions to the forthcoming inspection. The chapter draws on survey data from primary and secondary schools and material from our case studies. The data have been used to describe teachers' preparations and the strategies that heads develop to cope with the demands of the pre-inspection period and their effects on schools' prospects for improvement.

Chapter 4 describes the importance that school staff attach to the week of the inspection. It examines headteachers' management of the inspection week and the strategies which they employ in the hope of making the outcome as successful as possible. This chapter also discusses heads' views of their relationship with the inspectors and their assessment of the quality of their inspection team's judgements and of the feedback provided.

Chapter 5 looks at current practice in reporting key issues for action, at the key issues that are most frequently recommended by inspectors and at heads' reactions to the key issues in their school's inspection report. Heads' ability to anticipate their key issues is examined in some detail and the findings are analysed to see if they support the view that external inspection is, as is commonly believed, simply telling schools what they already know. The issue is seen as having particular significance because of its relevance to the later discussion of the reliability and usefulness of both school self-evaluation and 'self-inspection'.

Chapter 6 explores the inspection process through the eyes of newly appointed and established heads and the reactions of their staff. It notes that new heads, perhaps unsurprisingly, are more convinced of the value of inspection for school improvement and the chapter explores some of the reasons for this.

Chapter 7 examines the role of the governing body, particularly in the immediate aftermath of an inspection when governors find themselves with a legal obligation to produce a post-inspection action plan based on the key issues in the inspection report. The chapter describes the role that governors actually play during and after an inspection and discusses how the process has generally led to governors becoming more actively involved in schools. It also considers the difficulty that governors experience in performing their monitoring role and looks at the implications of this for 'self-inspection'.

The next chapter looks at heads' and RgIs' suggestions about the ways that OfSTED inspections might be improved. Their recommendations are reviewed in the light of the findings of the House of Commons Select Committee on *The Work of OfSTED* (House of Commons, 1999a) and their implications for the future development of the inspection process are discussed.

Chapter 9 draws on recent research and inspection evidence from the OfSTED database to comment on 'failing' schools and those with serious weaknesses. It also focuses on schools in socially disadvantaged locations and asks whether they have been treated fairly and whether further refinements to the comparative (benchmark) data, which enable inspectors to make comparisons and schools to set realistic targets, would serve a useful purpose.

The following chapter examines how the state of Victoria in Australia is tackling the challenge of school improvement and of making schools accountable for the quality of the education that they provide. This Australian model of school review is subjected to an analysis which provides new insights and a view of some possible directions for the future development of inspection in England.

Chapter 11 returns to the topics of self-evaluation and 'self-inspection' which were introduced earlier in this chapter. It discusses possible reasons for OfSTED's opposition to suggestions that these processes might become a formal part of the OfSTED system of inspection.

In the concluding chapter, we speculate about the possibilities and the disadvantages of a system of external inspection exclusively for the purposes of public accountability complemented by a parallel system of assisted 'self-inspection'. The latter would concentrate only on school improvement and have no accountability role. It would mean that OfSTED and the government would need to give greater trust to schools to assume responsibility for the 'self-inspection' of important aspects of their work that, at present, are externally inspected by OfSTED.

Notes

1. The system of inspection is slightly different in Wales and is administered by a separate office. The research reported in the book is based on English schools and the OfSTED system of inspection.

2

The OfSTED approach: a perspective

The purpose of this chapter is to make the approach adopted by the book a little more transparent. It is not meant to be an anti-OfSTED treatise or a defence of the current system. We try to take a perspective which is critical yet acknowledges the achievements of OfSTED since the implementation of the 1992 Education Act which established the Office for Standards in Education. We see OfSTED inspection as a constant, controlling influence on schools which has had positive effects and also some undesirable and unintended consequences. We are concerned about the reactions of teachers to inspection, its effect on development in schools and the nature of the role that heads, teachers and governors adopt during and after an inspection. The book is centrally concerned with the relationship between accountability and school improvement and we argue that the processes of passing judgement and providing support for improvement do not sit comfortably together and should be separated. We examine the part that schools can and, we believe, should play in inspection and discuss the challenge that OfSTED faces in adapting to changing attitudes and circumstances in schools which, we suggest, have implications for the future development of school inspection.

OfSTED's many achievements have to be set against what are seen as the main purposes of school inspection. OfSTED inspection provides a national evaluation of schools and information for the annual report of Her Majesty's Chief Inspector (HMCI). It ensures that individual schools are accountable for the standards they achieve, the quality of education they provide and the expenditure of taxpayers' money. Inspection also ensures that parents and the local community have access to information about their local schools and, through the identification of schools' strengths and weaknesses, it provides an opportunity for schools to act on the information in their inspection reports and thus to bring about improvements.

This book contributes to the debate about the extent to which OfSTED inspections are able to achieve all of these purposes. We shall begin by examining what we see as OfSTED's most important achievements.

The achievements of OfSTED

There are more than 18,600 state funded primary schools, around 1,000 special schools and over 3,600 secondary schools in England and between September 1993 and July 1998 all were inspected using a common framework which is available to schools (OfSTED, 1994/5). As a result of these inspections, the governing body of each school has received an inspection report providing a detailed analysis of the school's strengths and weaknesses and a list of key issues for action. All parents will have received at least a summary of the report's main findings.

The Inspection Framework – the latest revisions to which were published in late 1999 (OfSTED, 1999e) – is comprehensive, and although some heads and inspectors believe its scope is too wide, they did not use the opportunities provided by our surveys to suggest that important aspects had been missed or that the system required judgements to be made on the basis of inappropriate criteria.

OfSTED itself uses a variety of means to monitor and evaluate the work of inspection teams. Through its inspection quality division it has developed quality standards for contractors and inspectors, and an evaluation questionnaire is routinely sent to heads whenever an inspection has been completed. It also uses a system in which HMI 'drop in' at very short notice to monitor the inspectors' activities and to appraise critically a sample of reports. The number of such monitoring visits has increased to the extent that registered inspectors can expect to have their work examined at some point (*Update*, Autumn 1999).

The results of OfSTED's surveys have consistently demonstrated that heads are overwhelmingly satisfied with their school's inspection and view the experience positively. HMI monitoring has shown that very few inspections are conducted unprofessionally or without due regard to the OfSTED code of conduct and quality standards. Matthews *et al.* (1998) report that 94 per cent of schools accept their inspection team's judgements and believe that their inspection report is fair and accurate.

Our study of OfSTED inspections in secondary schools noted that almost three-quarters of the heads reported that their inspection had been fair (Fidler *et al.*, 1998). This positive view was confirmed by our primary school inspection survey which showed that just over three-quarters of the heads believed that the inspection had been fair and nine in every ten believed that they had formed good relationships with their registered inspector (RgI). Heads frequently added comments acknowledging the skills of their 'very astute', 'sensitive' and 'positive' inspectors but the word that was used most frequently to describe the RgIs was 'professional'. The evidence suggests that inspections are conducted by teams of inspectors who, in the main, prove to be sensitive and professional. The registered inspectors who lead inspection teams form good working relationships in schools and, when the inspection is complete, issue inspection reports that meet with the approval of a large majority of primary and secondary school heads. It should be recognised, however, that there are also examples of poor practice and a small number of inspectors have been de-registered.

The advent of inspection has generated a great deal more information about schools and their performance. This information is now in the public domain so that the database for government and for individual researchers and others has been greatly increased. Inspection has focused attention on standards and performance and on differences between schools with similar pupil intakes. For example, a school's performance and assessment data or PANDA (see Chapters 9 and 10) provides comparative (or benchmark) data for schools with similar proportions of pupils entitled to free school meals and (for primary schools) pupils with English as an additional language. It is now possible to identify differences between 'similar' schools that cannot be satisfactorily explained except by looking at such key factors as the quality of teaching and learning, and the effectiveness of leadership and management.

Inspection has also led to the identification of schools where the quality of education provided is not satisfactory and the system has made provision for additional support or special measures to be made (by HMI and LEA advisers) for these 'failing' schools. Heads, in all schools, are now given information about the quality of teaching (reports are given on individual teachers) and inspection reports include an assessment of the quality of leadership throughout the school.

OfSTED inspection has also provided heads and governors with a useful lever to encourage change – it can act as a catalyst – and to try to secure resources from the LEA. Schools with inadequate buildings and poor equipment can use the relevant criticisms in their inspection report to strengthen their case for additional expenditure. Similarly, those with pupils with 'significant emotional and behavioural difficulties' are urged to seek specialist support and to ensure that 'advice is available to staff concerning the management of these pupils' (OfSTED, 1999a, p.24). LEAs are also inspected and are judged, in part, on the quality of their support for schools, so they now have an even greater incentive to respond positively to heads' and governors' requests for funding and advice.

OfSTED's influence on schools' planning and development programmes has provided an opportunity for it to assume a role in continuing professional development. Some heads and teachers have completed inspector training courses and the Inspection Handbook is often described by heads as 'excellent in-service training'. OfSTED provides materials and accredits trainers for courses on 'self-inspection' (see Chapter 1), and publications such as *Planning Improvement* (OfSTED, 1995), *School Evaluation Matters* (OfSTED, 1998a) and *Lessons Learned from Special Measures* (OfSTED, 1999a) are full of practical advice for heads and teachers on a wide variety of topics.

OfSTED's considerable achievements have allowed it to make confident assertions about the strength of its approach, its role as a catalyst for change and the crucial part that external inspection plays in raising standards and improving schools. Its record seems to support the chief inspector's (HMCI) claim that 'schools in England are uniquely well placed to find answers' about their current strengths and weaknesses and the action they must take to achieve improvements and raise standards (see foreword to *School Evaluation Matters*, OfSTED, 1998a). Its effects on schools, however, extends far beyond these auditing and action planning processes and, as Chapter 1 suggested, include some long-term and pervasive influences on the way that teachers reflect on their own teaching and on the quality of education provided by their school.

The phases of inspection

Typically, in an average sized primary school, a lead inspector and a team of four other inspectors would begin their inspection on a Monday morning and leave before the end of the school day on the Thursday afternoon. In a large secondary school, a dozen or more inspectors might be involved in the inspection, and like those in primary schools, the inspection would usually be completed within one week. An inspection, however, is not a week-long event leading to the production of an inspection report. Most schools will from time to time speculate about the date of their next inspection and if they feel that the time is near might well begin their preparations before any formal announcement has been made. Our research into the impact of inspection found that the majority of secondary schools, in 1996, felt that they could delay preparations until official notification had been received. Recent reductions in the length of the period of notice (see Chapter 8) may imply a change of tactics because schools that want more than six to ten weeks of pre-inspection preparations must now attempt to anticipate the date of their reinspection. After the announcement of the date of an inspection, most schools undertake extensive preparations, review their practice, update their documents and begin to ensure that all the necessary paperwork is in place in time for the inspectors' arrival.

The inspection week itself is a critical time for staff and one which has a lasting effect on individual teachers and on the work of the school. Since September 1997, grades and individual feedback are routinely given at the end of the inspection to all the teaching staff who have been observed. Feedback on the outcomes of the inspection is given to the headteacher (frequently accompanied by the chair of governors) in a verbal report. The RgI usually makes arrangements to relay the findings to the full governing body at a later date.

Wide variations were found in the time it took schools to recover from 'inspection week' and generate the enthusiasm needed for post-OfSTED action planning. When a school has received its inspection report, its task is to focus on the key issues for action and the evidence in the report which supported their identification. It is through staff and governor analysis of these key issues and the report's supporting evidence that a school identifies the measures that are written into its action plan. However, the immediate post-inspection period can present schools with difficult management problems. The action plan may contain a programme of work that the head and governors are anxious to tackle. The stress and exhaustion that are often found in schools in the immediate aftermath of an inspection may have increased staff absence and mean that many teachers lack energy and find it difficult to motivate themselves to support the action planning process. Headteachers (including those in schools with 'good' reports) discovered in the immediate aftermath of an inspection that they needed to postpone their plans and concentrate on restoring staff morale and rekindling enthusiasm.

The inspection report not only provides governors and staff with key issues for inclusion in the school's post-inspection action plan but also informs parents about their children's school. When the main findings of reports are collated country-wide, they provide HMCI with data about trends in national standards and the effects of government initiatives such as the introduction of new curricula and teaching methods (e.g. the literacy hour).

In the period of two years or more after an action plan has been produced, schools usually make considerable efforts to address the key issues and implement the plan, particularly when they are seen as reflecting the school's priorities. The length of time taken to complete the action that the inspection report recommends can be a period of indeterminate length because there is no moment when, for example, standards have been raised sufficiently or teaching has been improved enough. The importance of action planning may finally rest with its influence on the school development or improvement plan (SDP/SIP) and the determination of targets that may remain priorities for the foreseeable future. In fact, in our 1997/1998 studies of reinspection in secondary schools, heads reported that they were not over-concerned about uncompleted key issues from their first inspection and explained the various reasons for this. There was, however, a tendency for the effects of inspection to fade after about 18 months and interest was not rekindled until a reinspection had been arranged.

Even when a reinspection was not due for some time, a school might need to make reference to the requirements of inspection, particularly when matters of school policy or changes in practice were being considered. Heads, staff and governors whose schools did not do well in their initial inspection would be likely to give careful consideration to the requirements of the Inspection Framework and avoid a repetition of the mistakes that led to the original criticisms. In this sense inspection can be seen as a process which not only has an impact between the pre-inspection preparation phase and the successful implementation of the post-OfSTED action plan, but also exerts a constant influence on the way that schools plan new developments. OfSTED is, we must conclude, a very powerful influence on most schools. As Jeffrey and Woods have pointed out:

The fact that OfSTED inspections are a mass project across all state schools . . . creates a climate within the education system in which the very concept of inspections becomes part of the 'education culture'. The idea of inspection in some shape or form has become part of the daily lives of schools (1998, p.2).

Inspectors' judgements

During 'inspection week', inspection teams aim to make judgements about educational standards and the strengths and weaknesses in teaching and other aspects of the schools' activities. The use of evidence to make judgements is now such a familiar process in schools that it is, perhaps, too readily taken for granted. It is a very demanding activity because inspectors are required to take account of so many facets of school life in a relatively brief time period. Their task is to make judgements on the basis of a variety of observations, discussions and the scrutiny of documents and pupils' work. This process of summarising qualitative judgements as a single number corresponding to a point on a rating scale is at the heart of OfSTED inspection.

The observation of teaching is a good example of the challenge that inspectors can expect to encounter in making judgements about a school. It is especially difficult because of the amount of information that the Framework suggests must be taken into account. Inspectors may have no more than 20 to 30 minutes in a classroom in which to apply a series of ratings to the quality of the various aspects of the lesson that they are observing. In a large secondary school, a teacher may be observed on no more than three occasions during 'inspection week'. In a small primary school, class teachers may be observed on more than one occasion every day, but it is unlikely that these lessons will have been seen from start to finish. The Parliamentary Select Committee on the work of OfSTED (House of Commons, 1999a) expressed a concern about the approach and commented:

We believe that the concerns expressed to us over inspectors observing only parts of lessons are justified. In some cases, observing only part of a lesson may not enable inspectors to make a proper assessment of teaching quality. This could contribute to a false impression of the overall quality of teaching in the school (paragraph 87).

In its response to the Select Committee's recommendations, the government (House of Commons, 1999c) appeared to endorse these findings (p.8) but did not express a view on the desirability of observing lessons in their entirety. OfSTED's response was more forthright: 'It is not the case that a full lesson must be seen every time nor that seeing a part of a lesson prevents the inspector from making a valid judgement about the quality of teaching' (House of Commons, 1999c, p.24).

OfSTED and the Select Committee have simply agreed to differ on whether part or whole lessons should be observed and it is almost certain that OfSTED will not now instruct inspectors to make any significant changes to their current practice. Whether inspectors observe entire lessons or parts of lessons is not the only and probably not the most important issue to consider. The large number of very detailed and often difficult decisions which are listed in Table 2.1 are likely to be problematic in either case. They are also likely to increase the probability that inspectors will rate teachers on the various criteria according to their general impression of the teachers' overall effectiveness. This 'halo effect', as it is usually called, creates spuriously high consistency between judges' ratings of different criteria applied to the assessment of the same person. For OfSTED inspectors, it probably represents a sensible strategy for coping with a surprising plethora of detailed information which must be speedily synthesised from a relatively small sample of a teacher's classroom behaviour.

The nature of the OfSTED judgement process is determined by the highly concentrated and very intense nature of an inspection. It is an experience that places inspectors under great pressure because they have to complete their observations and discussions, and prepare oral feedback on the outcomes of the inspection within three to five days of their arrival in the school. Among the primary and secondary schools involved in our research, there were few expressions of surprise at the nature of the process and, as we have already noted, a large number of complimentary comments about the 'professionalism' of RgIs and their inspection teams.

Power and obedience

The chief inspector has noted that headteachers frequently treat the key issues in their inspection reports as if they were a set of instructions which they were obliged to follow. He added 'It is not a mandatory programme of action. A school may well decide that a particular key issue is not the issue that it wishes to pursue at that moment' (*Times Educational Supplement*, 14 May 1999). Every head and chair of governors understands that the production of an action plan is a statutory obligation upon the school's governing body. The fact that the implementation of that plan is a voluntary activity and that action planned on key issues can be ignored is not so widely publicised. The chief inspector's invitation to heads to exercise professional judgement may have come as a considerable surprise to the staff and governors in many schools. Some may worry about the implications of the phrase 'at that moment' in HMCI's remarks and most will be aware that an important focus for reinspection is 'progress on the key issues from the previous inspection'. Few are so disingenuous that they would fail to consider the possible consequences of a decision to ignore several of their key issues. In the same article, however, the chief inspector explains:

> It is the school, and only the school, which must take responsibility for its own decisions. To argue otherwise is to travel down a road which leads to a loss of autonomy and the professional demoralisation which inevitably follows.

Table 2.1   A summary of the judgements used by OfSTED inspectors in the evaluation of a lesson

---

Teaching
- Did the teacher appear to have a good understanding of the subject?
- Did the teacher appear to have expectations of pupils' attainments which were high enough to be challenging but not so high that they were too demanding for some of the pupils in the class?
- Did the teacher use the evidence of classroom questions, observations and other assessments during the lesson to adapt the teaching to children's needs?
- Did the teacher meet the needs of pupils with different levels of previous learning by providing tasks and explanations that were appropriate?
- Was the teacher's planning for this lesson effective and did it fit well into the planned curriculum?
- Was there evidence that the planning for this lesson had been informed by the assessment of pupils' earlier work?
- Did the teaching strategies and classroom organisation match the lesson objectives and the children's needs?
- Were pupils managed well? Were they well behaved?
- Were time and resources used effectively during the lesson?
- Was homework set and, if so, was it used effectively to reinforce and extend the learning that had taken place during the lesson?

Overall was the teacher's performance:

1	2	3	4	5	6	7
excellent	very good	good	satisfactory	unsatisfactory	poor	very poor

Response
- Did the pupils concentrate on their work and was their interest in the lesson sustained?
- Were pupils developing a capacity for personal study?
- Were they courteous and trustworthy? Did they show respect for others?
- Did the pupils get on well together and co-operate effectively?
- Did they form constructive relationships and, where relevant, contribute to racial harmony?
- Did they show respect for other pupils' feelings, values and beliefs?

Overall were pupils' attitudes to their work:

1	2	3	4	5	6	7
excellent	very good	good	satisfactory	unsatisfactory	poor	very poor

Attainment
- What did pupils know and understand about the subject?
- What proportion achieve or exceed the expectations of the National Curriculum?
- Are there variations in the attainments of boys and girls or of pupils from different ethnic backgrounds?
- How does the attainment of pupils compare with national averages?

Overall were pupils' attainments:

1	2	3
well above average	about average	well below average

Progress
- Was reinforcement of previous learning or extension of previous learning in evidence during the lesson? If so what was being reinforced/extended and how effectively?
- Was there evidence of new learning taking place and progress being made?
- Was good progress made by high, average and low attaining pupils and those with special educational needs?
- Were there differences in the rates of progress of boys, girls or those for whom English is an additional language?

Overall was progress:

1	2	3	4	5	6	7
excellent	very good	good	satisfactory	unsatisfactory	poor	very poor

Other evidence might include, if appropriate, pupils' competence in reading, writing, speaking and listening, evidence of curricular planning, the use of resources, accommodation and support teachers or other adults in the classroom.

This is a very interesting point of view and one that seems in tune with the views of Michael Fullan and others which are discussed later in this chapter. However, many and perhaps even most teachers believe that OfSTED inspectors are not making suggestions but are imposing requirements which must be met.

In schools, anxiety about the inspection findings meant that they were often addressed 'too obediently'. Heads generally felt insecure about rejecting key issues although experienced school leaders (see Chapter 6) were more inclined to reject those that were not in accord with their perceptions of the school's values. Schools did not want their development to be seen as entirely due to the pressures of OfSTED, though they did agree that the approaching reinspection had speeded up the implementation of change. Development planning, for example, was sometimes perceived to be of little importance, but those heads facing a reinspection ensured that their key issues were adequately addressed in time for the inspectors' visit.

Schools' responses to inspection

Our research also noted that schools varied in the extent to which they felt their management processes were in tune with what they saw as the 'OfSTED ideal'. Some heads commented that the Framework was an excellent management manual, while others defied what they perceived to be an 'orthodoxy'. The responses of secondary schools to inspection were placed in three categories (see Ouston, Fidler and Earley, 1998). The 'developing/reflective' school was, at least, adequately managed and had acceptable levels of pupil attainment. The inspection could be said to have had little impact because the usual outcome was for these schools to be told to continue to extend current practice. Most of the secondary schools in our surveys came into this category. The 'complacent' school was popular with its community and had a relatively socially advantaged intake and above average examination results. It was usually fairly traditional in its approach and had an enthusiastic parent body. The 'struggling school' typically served a disadvantaged community and felt that it would never meet what it perceived to be the 'OfSTED ideal'.

In the medium term (a period of one to two years after the inspection), most schools achieved the implementation of at least some of the key issues in the action plan but there were wide variations in schools' response to the inspection. In the opinion of some headteachers, circumstances can not only hamper progress in the medium term but make it unwise, for a variety of reasons, to give priority to the provisions of the action plan. Progress at 'complacent' and 'struggling' schools was often related to perceptions of the competence and quality of their inspectors and schools' faith in the validity of their key issues. 'Struggling' schools, often in areas of social and economic deprivation (see Chapter 9), were demoralised by criticisms from inspection teams and sometimes expressed the belief that their inspection team had been less than fully competent. 'Complacent' schools generally expected to receive a good inspection report. Those who had their achievements recognised but also had new issues raised for their attention were likely to be given a mandate for action by the inspection.

The question arises, therefore, whether the disruption to schools caused by inspection is necessary. It might be argued that inspection's undesirable side effects represent the price that must be paid if educational standards are to be raised. However, it is also necessary to ask whether the inspection process needs to rely so heavily on external judgements about the performance of individual heads and teachers in a single week in their professional lives. Are the right people being asked to make these judgements in the right set of circumstances? Such questions need to be asked from time to time because government faith in the inspection process may become such a powerful creed that teachers assume that OfSTED-style inspections are the best or perhaps the only means by which schools can be prompted to improve. OfSTED may also become complacent and begin to believe that the best possible approach to inspection has already been devised and while matters of detail might be changed from time to time, there is no need to consider anything too fundamental.

There are alternative approaches and, as we will later argue, the dominance of the 'OfSTED orthodoxy' and the pressure that it exerts on schools to take account of the OfSTED criteria is limiting.

MacBeath, commenting on the blend of pressure and support that would facilitate school improvement and bring benefits to schools, remarks:

> So, the optimum balance has to be finely judged depending on the circumstances of the school. That is why the routine OfSTED or OHMCI cycle of inspections is inefficient and ill informed. It treats schools as if their needs and skills were all the same (1999, p.3).

It is a point that receives some support from the Select Committee.

> There is a broad spectrum of activity stretching from detailed advice – telling the school what to do – at one end, and a wholly 'hands-off' audit at the other. The point along the spectrum at which inspectors should work will depend upon the individual circumstances of the school. A more confident school may require a response from their inspection team which is closer to the 'audit' end of this spectrum, while other schools may benefit from a response which is closer to the 'advice' end (House of Commons, 1999a, para 98, p.34).

The possibility of such flexibility of response is not formally part of the OfSTED process which prides itself in applying 'rigour' and 'robust judgements' in much the same way in all schools whatever their circumstances. Dean Fink (1999), a visiting Canadian academic, expressed amazement at the toughness of the approach in England and its emphasis on blame rather than encouragement and support for struggling schools.

In many parts of Europe, the system of school inspection appears to be less personal and less threatening. Government agencies have moved the focus for school inspection from individual pupil and teacher performance to the performance of the school (see Kogan, 1999; Dalin, 1998; Hopes, 1997; St John Brookes, 1997; Gois, 1998; Altrichter and Specht, 1998; Webb *et al.*, 1998). When the school as a whole is the unit for inspection, its effectiveness might be reviewed by looking at such things as curriculum development, strategic and improvement planning, staff development, and the provision for particular groups of pupils or subjects. An assessment of the school's monitoring procedures and its record in implementing the outcomes of self-evaluation are likely to be important features. This would be very different from an OfSTED inspection and would be largely, but not entirely, 'a paper-based audit trail' supplemented by discussions with the headteacher, governors and members of staff. Inspectors would not usually have a role in the direct assessment of the standards achieved by pupils nor in the inspection of the quality of individual teachers. An alternative approach to 'school review', practised in Victoria, Australia is analysed in some detail in Chapter 10.

We are aware, however, of a large number of overseas governments that are interested in the 'English approach' to inspection. Many have sent representatives to London for discussions with OfSTED's International Division and OfSTED representatives have visited other countries where they have given presentations and advised Ministers of Education. If the OfSTED inspection model is being exported, it is possible that other countries may decide to modify their own systems in the light of OfSTED's advice. This could mean that there will be an increasing emphasis, internationally, on evaluation and control mechanisms; checks on statutory requirements; the identification of poorly performing teachers and the public exposure of weak and failing schools. However, visitors from England to other countries in Europe and elsewhere would probably find themselves being persuaded of the merits of an inspectorate that provides advice and support and undertakes the meta-evaluation of schools' self-evaluation.

Prescribing change

In his well-known book, Fullan (1991) discusses the process of change in schools in North America and although written about a decade ago, his work is still relevant and provides a critical perspective on externally driven, OfSTED-like approaches to school improvement. He points out that changes are often handed to teachers who are perhaps already struggling to cope with the considerable daily demands of the classroom and its routine and unexpected challenges. External pressure is resisted to avoid additional disruption that could threaten to make teaching an intolerably stressful occupation. This analysis suggests that it is important for inspectors to be aware of the implications of their recommendations for change and to judge whether the school's daily routines can cope with the implications of the post-

OfSTED action plan. Visiting inspection teams may not always be in a strong position to do this and may not know whether their suggestions for doing things differently necessarily represent an improvement. Fullan suggests that external agencies recommending reforms should help to implement them and should be capable of winning the support of the teaching staff. He argues that change of this kind can only be effective in schools when the external agent and the staff have a shared vision, develop a working group that understands the implications of the proposed change and arrange continuing follow-up and external support. Without these essential ingredients, change is unlikely to be successfully sustained. Whether Fullan's concerns are equally applicable to prescriptions resulting from the diagnosis of individual schools' weaknesses is an interesting question (Fidler, Russell and Simkins 1997, p.64).

It is possible, for example, that inspectors of an inner city school in a disadvantaged area might not themselves have managed a school in such circumstances or taught pupils whose everyday lives are beset with severe difficulties. We suggest (in Chapter 9) that such schools are more likely than those in stable communities to be judged harshly. OfSTED inspection is a 'hands-off' process and because inspectors do not help to implement their recommendations they have few opportunities to learn about such schools or grasp the implications of the specific proposals made in the school's inspection report. Nevertheless, although there is nothing in the OfSTED process which provides such experience, inspectors may have gained it acting in other professional capacities. Schools ought to recognise that they should consider the findings of their inspection report critically, but this is difficult when the 'recommendations' are made by a body which appears to play such a pivotal role in teachers' professional lives.

Fullan's message that reform cannot simply be mandated has many echoes in the earlier work of Paulo Freire (1973) who warned of the practical and political implications of transplanting solutions and the tendency of those on whom solutions are imposed 'to give in to disheartenment and feelings of inferiority'. He concludes:

> But since these borrowed solutions are neither generated by a critical analysis of the context itself, nor adequately adapted to the context, they prove inoperable and unfruitful (p.13).

Heads and teachers it seems, in their responses to our surveys and case study interviews, are not as concerned about 'borrowed solutions' as are university researchers and academics. As already noted, OfSTED inspections have won general acceptance and are perceived as a necessary accountability mechanism. Their role in school improvement, however, is more problematic. The crucial point is about the adequacy of the diagnosis to know whether the solution is appropriate and whether it will work.

This perspective on OfSTED inspection helps to explain why the concept of the 'self-inspecting' school is believed to be important. We have argued in these opening chapters that OfSTED can be seen as a controlling agent exerting its influence in a variety of ways to help bring about changes that reflect government policy as well as good practice in teaching and the management and leadership of schools. However, it might also be argued that except for 'failing' schools where the sanctions and pressures are great, a school's response to its inspection can be variable and is determined, at least in theory if not in practice, by its accountability to the governing body (see Chapter 7).

Schools have learned to cope with the process of inspection as a social activity. They greet members of their inspection teams with 'a positive outlook', the appearance of confidence, a professional friendliness, a degree of deference, some disguised apprehension and considerable concern for their comfort and well-being. There are fewer rules about how heads and teachers should engage with the process professionally, how they might adopt an OfSTED perspective of their own, how to assert a degree of independence or a capacity for critical reflection about the school. The process leaves little room for manoeuvre and few opportunities for a level of involvement among school staff that would aid their understanding or support the growth of skills in self-evaluation. The following four chapters which look at the pre-inspection preparation period, the week of the inspection, the post-inspection period and the reactions of heads and inspectors to the OfSTED process, spell out some of the implications of the model of inspection that has been developed.

3

Pre-inspection preparations and school development

In the current drive towards school improvement and the raising of standards, inspection is seen as a crucial element in the national strategy. However, the ground is shifting and the sense in which inspection is believed to be important has been subject to change. This is certainly true of the 'pre-inspection preparation period' which, it could be argued, was initially intended to act as a catalyst for development by prompting schools to identify their weaknesses and bring about improvements in readiness for the inspectors' arrival. Periods of notice of a year or more were quite often reported in our primary and secondary school surveys that were conducted between 1994 and 1998. These lengthy notice periods were presumably arranged so that schools would have sufficient time to undertake major reviews and to try out new systems and policies. The length of the period of notice has been cut to twelve weeks or less and there is no longer the same emphasis on the immediate pre-inspection period as a catalyst for school improvement. This chapter will argue that the value of the pre-inspection period has been undermined.

Consultants and 'dry run' inspections

Nearly all schools prepare thoroughly for an inspection. Our data showed that the vast majority of schools took the opportunity to undertake a review of the quality of their activities. Most headteachers believed their review had been thorough and more than one in ten primary schools had used LEA advisers, inspectors or other consultants to undertake a full review of the school's activities. Around 70 per cent had used advisers and consultants to undertake a partial review. The use of consultants to help secondary schools to prepare for inspection was just as common and has increased considerably since 1993. A quarter of the secondary schools surveyed in 1993 used an external consultant to help them to prepare for inspection. This rose to just over a third in 1994 and to three-quarters of the secondary school sample in 1996. This rising trend might well continue as local education authority inspections by OfSTED make LEAs more concerned about the outcomes of school inspections and more likely to persuade schools to employ advisers to support their pre-inspection preparations.

In both primary and secondary schools there were examples of head-teachers who had organised 'dry run' inspections. One secondary·head had invited a full inspection team to visit the school and take each department through the inspection process and then work with them on their weaknesses. A head of faculty in a case study school welcomed the opportunity to have:

> Another professional who is working in the field and knows what they are talking about and is committed to the process of teaching and learning, coming in and having a look at the way we are doing it. I found that incredibly useful.

The headteacher and governors of an urban primary school had made simi-lar arrangements for an equally thorough pre-inspection review that was conducted by a team of experienced inspectors led by an ex-HMI. The head was convinced that the exercise, and the intensive efforts that the staff had made to address the weaknesses that the mock inspection had uncovered, had 'rescued' the school from almost certain failure.

Elaborate preparations and the use of resources to employ consultants and advisers has been criticised by OfSTED who argue that the task of inspecting a school and identifying its strengths and weaknesses is theirs and theirs alone. Rose (1995), who was Director of Inspections, noted that preparations for inspection are often very expensive and take the form of a 'pre-inspection inspection' in which advice is provided to prepare the school for the 'real thing'. He recommended that heads and governors should not invest in elaborate preparations because it is the purpose of the inspection team to identify strengths and weaknesses. Schools, he believed, should prepare to get as much benefit as possible from inspection that is 'not an end in itself' and should not require 'an expensive dress rehearsal'.

The OfSTED booklet *Making the Most of Inspection* (1998b) advises heads and governors that:

> There is little evidence that external trial inspections improve inspection per-formance. Many teachers report that they increase stress, set false hares run-ning and disrupt the normal function of the school. We believe that external trial inspections are a waste of money.

The message is repeated by the chief inspector in his fifth annual report (OfSTED, 1999b) which complains about LEAs that:

> continue to divert significant amounts of scarce resources to pre-inspection advice and 'support' partly because schools ask for it and partly because both LEAs and schools want to ensure a favourable report. About half the LEAs inspected provided a significant amount of support to schools before their OfSTED inspection, but there was little evidence that such support promoted real improvement in the schools (p.72, paragraph 351).

These comments suggest that headteachers and staff, who are working closely with LEA advisers and consultants in order to avoid being criticised in a forthcoming inspection, are less capable than OfSTED inspectors alone of providing heads and governors with a useful assessment of their strengths and weaknesses. However, our evidence shows that in 1993 most OfSTED inspections were conducted in schools which were inspected by their own or neighbouring LEA teams. In 1997/8 a small number of large contracting firms dominated but our 1998 survey of registered inspectors discovered that 40 per cent of RgIs were conducting OfSTED inspections as an integral part of their work for an LEA and many more were ex-LEA advisers who were now working for contractors. It is not clear, therefore, why LEA staff or former LEA staff working with schools to prepare them for inspection should be thought to be less capable of providing effective audits and worthwhile recommendations about school improvements.

OfSTED's opposition to trial inspections is also difficult to reconcile with the assertion that 'Headteachers should know their school better than anyone else' (OfSTED, 1998a, p.8). OfSTED has doubts about the extent to which heads, governors, teachers and LEAs can be trusted to uncover the truth about their schools. The debate has important implications for the future of self-evaluation and its place, if any, within the system of inspection and the issue is discussed in more detail in Chapter 11.

It is helpful for the OfSTED (1998a) booklet *School Evaluation Matters* to offer detailed advice about the conduct of self-evaluations that can be carried out in the years between schools' OfSTED inspections. However, there are ambivalent feelings about the validity of heads', governors' and teachers' judgements and there are, as yet, no plans nationally either to ensure that all schools have adequate self-evaluation skills or to allow 'self-inspection' to influence the outcomes of the 'official' inspection process. Equally puzzling is the fact that the 'high stakes' of inspection are not acknowledged in the debate about trial inspections. Many heads faced with even the remote possibility of a very public failure or of making the 'mistake' of wasting scarce resources on unnecessary consultants would have little doubt that the sensible course of action is do everything possible to avoid a damaging 'defeat'. There should be no surprise, therefore, that schools' preparations are elaborate and divert resources that might otherwise have been available for other purposes including the provision of resources for pupils.

Anticipating criticisms

Our survey of primary schools that were about to be inspected in 1998 asked heads whether they had identified shortcomings that they felt would be adversely commented upon when the inspection took place. Those that identified weaknesses were asked why they would not have been addressed in readiness for the inspection. More than eight out of ten primary heads believed that they knew of weaknesses that were about to attract adverse comments. Most explained that their inability to avoid these anticipated criticisms was the result of a lack of time, a lack of money for equipment or because of staffing difficulties. (Heads explained, for example, that they had 'no co-ordinator', 'NQTs requiring support', 'staff absences', 'inherited problems from the previous head', 'too many teaching commitments', 'a disciplinary action pending', 'no time to train new staff', 'lack of appropriate subject expertise' and so on.) Some heads suggested that the introduction of government initiatives explained why, in their view, there would be insufficient time to put things right. The most common comment, in 1998, was that the 'literacy hour' was an urgent priority and, therefore, a reason for delay. However, other government initiatives (for example, the numeracy project) had also supplanted current plans.

Typical comments from primary school heads were:

> We have put the foundation subjects on hold as the National Curriculum has been altered and we await new guidelines. RE is on hold because the LEA is due to publish a new approved syllabus.

> New government initiatives will force this back still further (the school believed that its lack of development of design and technology would be criticised).

> Target setting and baseline assessment issues have taken time away from other SDP issues (an explanation of why a number of issues were expected to lead to critical comment).

Urgent action or rational planning?

The views of headteachers who felt that their schools would be criticised for low standards of attainment were instructive. Heads expressed the view that raising the level of pupils' attainments in, for example, English or mathematics was a particularly long-term aim with no end in sight and no immediate prospects of improvement. Headteachers see higher standards arising as the culmination of long-term curriculum developments and overall improvements to the quality of teaching which are achieved as a result of careful strategic planning, improved resources and programmes of staff development. There was an emphasis on doing 'a proper job' but the number of elements of the strategy that heads believed had to be in place before progress could be made seemed to place the target out of reach. There were to be no urgent actions or 'short-term fixes to achieve national standards' because such matters are 'ongoing processes' or as one primary head explained: 'They are long-term issues, planned in the SDP. We don't intend to address them by a knee-jerk reaction'. Their stance demonstrates the extent to which schools have placed their faith in the model of rational planning which is implicit in the OfSTED inspection model and in the current emphasis on school development plans, post-OfSTED action planning and target-setting. This 'common sense' point of view seemed, rightly or wrongly, to have ensured that the prospects for immediate improvements were bleak and to have redefined urgent action to address weaknesses in children's learning as a new category of 'unwise' behaviour. Planned delay, the need to prioritise, tackling issues in a predetermined order and avoiding wasting time on matters which the government may be about to change were constant themes and served as an explanation for lengthy planning processes which aimed to ensure that the quality of provision would be high when the plans were finally implemented.

> We need to review this area carefully, monitor new strategies carefully and take measured steps to reach our target. We don't want to rush into anything because OfSTED are coming (primary headteacher).

In their responses to our survey, headteachers often made it clear that the pre-inspection period was not the time to concentrate upon school-wide improvements. Their view is supported by the Centre for the Study of Comprehensive Schools whose broadsheet giving advice to schools about inspection (CSCS, 1994) contained a section entitled 'Tips unwise and useful'. There was only one 'unwise tip' which was to warn teachers that they should not 'contemplate major changes to school practices and policies' before an inspection. It is advice that has the wholehearted support of the majority of heads in primary schools. Some secondary schools used the time to bring about changes which would reduce the number of weaknesses likely to be identified by their inspection team but, as in primary schools, most secondary heads, and particularly those who had been in post for some time, assembled their paperwork but did not make major changes before the inspection.

Activity in the pre-inspection period

Headteachers' views

The announcement of an impending inspection galvanises schools into action. About one in three heads in primary and secondary schools felt that their inspection had *not* affected the pace of development but one-half of the primary and one-third of the secondary heads reported that change and development in the school had been speeded up by the announcement that an inspection was about to take place. However, 15 per cent of primary heads and one-third of secondary heads felt that development had been hindered and they claimed that the need to prepare for the inspection had 'knocked improvement sideways', 'slowed us up' and 'stopped us in our tracks' and, as one primary head explained, 'We suspended development to prepare for inspection'. When we asked the Spring 1997 cohort of primary school heads to rate the extent to which pre-inspection preparation had made a contribution to school development, only one-quarter of the heads then expressed optimism about the influence of the pre-inspection period on school development, while 28 per cent indicated that their preparations for inspection had made 'little' or 'no contribution'. More than four in ten had doubts and some schools now had serious reservations about the usefulness of the preparation period.

> We (the head and deputy head) spent month after month doing silly stuff while the priorities which we had were put on hold. Perhaps unwisely! The mind-set of the staff; their concerns about inspection; the need to train them to cope with an inspector in their room. It all took time. OfSTED came along and said, 'The stuff you have put on hold is the stuff you need'. It held us back by about a year (deputy head of a primary school).

In 1996, three in ten secondary school heads had rated the value of inspection preparations highly. This was similar to the result obtained from the 1997 primary survey but a much lower figure than the earlier secondary school surveys had indicated (Ouston, Fidler and Earley, 1998). Inspection was undoubtedly a catalyst for activity in every school but it is how heads perceive the value of that activity that probably accounts for most of the variation in their responses. Teachers generally worked very hard and some became exhausted by the additional tasks which they felt were required. Exactly what staff were doing to prepare for inspection and how their activity affected the development of the school were questions which we investigated.

Headteachers' reports of busy preparations, stress and hard work are amply illustrated by the comments of primary school teachers who were interviewed about one year after their inspection. They reported late evenings in their classrooms, a sharpened sense of camaraderie amongst the staff and the sacrifice of weekends, half-term breaks and family and leisure activities. Heads sympathised with individual members of staff who wanted time and the opportunity to make sure that the quality of their teaching did not become the subject of adverse criticism. One head commented that, no developments or changes were made in 'OfSTED year' so the staff could concentrate on teaching and not be 'burnt out' for the inspection. Another explained that 'it takes time to move staff forward in their expectations and to work in more collaborative ways', and a primary head, referring to weaknesses which he felt would attract adverse comment from the inspection team, commented: 'Historical aspects of the school put other aspects in front of these.' Perhaps the cryptic 'Can't change history!' summed up the feelings of heads who explained their policy of inaction by emphasising the importance of being sensitive to the culture of the school and recognising teachers' need for support at a particularly anxious time. This comment from a head in an inner city primary school revealed how heads can feel a little like spectators while teachers enact their own busy agendas. 'Staff were overplanning. Everything was pinned down. I was worried that they might boil over. It took the sparkle and buzz from teaching.'

The teachers' views

Teachers in the case studies of primary schools provided remarkably similar descriptions of the way they spent their time in the inspection preparation phase (the period of notice varied from two to fifteen months). Activities included the production of displays for classroom walls and the school corridors, rehearsals to get used to having an inspector in the room, checking through children's books, embellishing marking which may not have been done thoroughly at the time, updating records and improving those that were incomplete, working on the individual education plans of pupils with special needs, making resources for use in OfSTED week, tidying cupboards and ensuring that materials were well organised and clearly labelled. A great deal of time was spent in detailed lesson planning not only for the inspection week itself but also for the weeks and months leading up to it. Lesson plans were revised, reviewed, discussed with colleagues and anxiously revised again, but the exercise seemed artificial and unreal to teachers and illustrated the impossibility of achieving the level of perfection for which they seemed to be striving. It was, understandably, a difficult time and teachers' energies seemed to be directed at covering all the possibilities and ensuring that they were not 'found out'. A co-ordinator suggested:

> If we had not had it we might just have skated along really. OfSTED gave us a bit of a shock and we thought we'd better do those folders, we'd better make sure that the classroom is the way it should be. I'd better make sure I have done all my record keeping (science co-ordinator in a primary school).

The core co-ordinators found it difficult to estimate the amount of time which might be spent on the preparation of lessons, but it was clear that some were spending many hours over a period of months preparing lessons which they hoped would come to a climax of near perfection in 'OfSTED week'.

In most schools, teachers visited each others' classrooms, often late into the evening, to provide encouragement and offer help. Preparations for inspection and the rituals which were created around the process were a rich source of illustrations which were indelibly etched in teachers' memories. They provided an important complement to the viewpoint of the primary school heads who had suggested that external pressures and a lack of resources had prevented the schools from achieving developments which would help them to avoid adverse comments from the inspectors. Teachers' anxiety about their fate at the hands of the inspection team and their instinct for self-preservation meant that they were unwilling to embark upon major development of this kind.

A maths co-ordinator in an urban primary school provided a very detailed commentary on the preparation period which not only identified her priorities and those of her colleagues but gave a sense of what it might mean 'to boil over' in the months before an inspection.

> Preparation was a very intense, almost frantic time. We were trying to get everything as perfect as we could. Which children will they hear read? What displays? If it's not in front of their noses, they might not notice. It was all part of the big build-up. Not just for inspection week. You felt they are going to want to see those books from the previous term. They are going to want to see all their work. We even planned what we would have on the walls that week. We were planning months ahead and we would say, 'Right we'll save that until next term so the inspectors will see it' . . . We don't want to go through that again just yet (mathematics co-ordinator in a primary school).

A science co-ordinator in an inner-city school described how hard she and her colleagues worked in the pre-inspection period but a year later had come to a realisation of the limitations of the achievements of inspection preparations.

> We over-planned. It was panic mode again. The planning period was unproductive. You were thinking, 'Have I done this? Have I done that? Is this right? Are they going to like this?' Getting my IEPs (individual education plans for pupils with special educational needs) up to date and more detailed – that was good but the detailed planning was a terrible mistake. We wasted our time (science co-ordinator in a primary school).

Schools which attempt major changes

Earlier, we noted that most headteachers did not attempt new initiatives as part of their inspection preparations. Three-quarters of the primary heads preferred what they considered to be a 'minor change' or 'no change' strategy and acted as if the pre-inspection period was not the right time to embark upon major school development.

The survey data were collapsed to form two categories by adding the 'major' and 'fairly major' change schools together and similarly amalgamating the 'minor' change and 'no change' schools. These data (see Table 3.1) were used to identify four types of school distinguished simply by the amount of change they had attempted in the pre-inspection period and their headteachers' feelings about the schools' state of preparedness. Thus, there were schools that had attempted 'major' or 'fairly major' changes that felt ready for inspection and those that still felt unprepared. In the same way, 'minor/no change' schools were also divided into those that did and did not feel prepared for inspection. Table 3.1 shows how each of these four school types expected to be judged during their inspection week. A large majority of schools made few changes in the pre-inspection period and they expected to be more successful than schools that attempted major changes.

Complete information was available on 342 primary schools but only 24 per cent (81 schools) had attempted 'major' or 'fairly major' changes and only about one in six of them (14) predicted that their major changes would be rewarded with a good inspection report. Their lack of optimism

Table 3.1 Pre-inspection preparations and heads' expectations

	Group 1 Major changes not yet prepared	Group 2 Major changes well prepared	Group 3 Minor changes not yet prepared	Group 4 Minor changes well prepared
Expects report to be 'poor' or 'very poor'	17% (7)	10% (4)	5% (3)	1% (2)
Expects report to be 'satisfactory'	76% (32)	62% (24)	65% (40)	41% (82)
Expects report to be 'good' or 'very good'	7% (3)	28% (11)	31% (19)	58% (115)
Totals	42	39	62	199

Survey B1: Total cases = 342; missing data = 28.

suggested that many in this group had embarked on major developments in an attempt to avoid failure. The third group had not attempted to change very much and felt unprepared for inspection but were a slightly more confident group than the well-prepared major change schools. The fourth group of schools opted for minimum change in the months before inspection and believed that they were well prepared. More than one-half of them (58 per cent) predicted that they would be judged to be 'good' or 'very good'. If the views of headteachers are correct, the relatively small number of schools which had undertaken major development should include a larger than expected proportion of failing schools and those with poor reports.

Table 3.2 makes use of the follow-up survey data to find out whether schools that attempted 'major changes' in the pre-inspection period did, in fact, receive poorer inspection reports than those that adopted a minimal change strategy. Table 3.2 compares heads' perceptions of the extent of development (assessed before the inspection took place) according to their

Table 3.2 Pre-inspection school development and its relationship to the outcomes of inspection

	Major changes	Fairly major changes	Minor changes	No changes
Judged to be 'poor' or 'very poor'	0%	9% (5)	8% (15)	8% (2)
Judged to be 'satisfactory'	47% (8)	29% (16)	22% (44)	27% (7)
Judged to be 'good' or 'very good'	53% (9)	62% (34)	71% (141)	65% (17)
Totals	17	55	200	26

Total number of cases = 298; missing data = 13.

overall opinion of the report which was received after the inspection. (Heads rated their reports on a five point scale – 'very poor' to 'very good'.)

Schools that undertook 'major changes' in the run-up to an inspection avoided failure (in the form of poor reports). Those that undertook 'fairly major changes' were, despite their lack of confidence, as successful as schools that made no attempt to improve in the pre-inspection period. The 'minor change' schools were the most successful in obtaining a 'good' or 'very good' report. It is interesting to compare the lack of confidence in the outcome of the inspection of the 'major change' schools (see Table 3.1) with the final outcome summarised in Table 3.2.

When heads were asked whether they were 'pleased' or 'disappointed' with the outcome of their inspection, a quarter of the 'minor change' and 28 per cent of the 'no change' heads reported disappointment, but the corresponding figures for the 'major change' and 'fairly major change' groups were 11 and 18 per cent respectively. Despite the widespread reluctance to see the pre-inspection period as a spur to action, those who did act seemed to have their efforts acknowledged and their fears for the outcome of their inspection were not realised.

The OfSTED handbook

Teachers' understanding of the OfSTED handbook might seem to be crucial to their experiences of success or disappointment during an inspection. For example, an emphasis on displaying pupils' work on classroom walls might have less influence on inspectors' judgements than measures to improve the quality of teaching or extra attention to literacy, numeracy, target-setting and the attainments and progress of minority groups and pupils with special educational needs. All of these are matters that have been declared to be important (see OfSTED, 1997a). A careful reading of other schools' inspection reports might, for example, have led to schools giving an increased emphasis to the development of monitoring, assessment and provision for information technology. An impending inspection can be seen as the start of a game in which skilful players will seek out the information that will enhance their chances of obtaining a good report. Those who, for a variety of reasons, refuse to 'play the system' may approach the inspection without seeking such 'advantages'.

We wondered whether the importance that heads attached to the inspection handbook (OfSTED, 1994/5) influenced the outcome of inspection and whether heads perceived training as an OfSTED inspector to be a significant advantage to the school. Wilkinson and Howarth (1996) discovered that teachers' responses generally indicated a lack of understanding of the purposes of inspection and concluded that it was important to encourage teachers to get to know the OfSTED Framework. They suggested dividing the handbook among staff and ensuring that every member of staff had a very detailed understanding of at least one section.

When heads were asked about the importance they attached to the OfSTED handbook, only three per cent considered it to be of 'little' or 'no importance' and, in 1997, some had not even acquired a copy for their school. A third of heads thought that it was only of 'some importance' to inspection preparations but most felt that it was 'important' or 'very important' to make use of the handbook to guide preparations for inspection. Nearly one in ten primary school heads were qualified inspectors or had a member of staff in the school who was either a qualified inspector or who was currently completing OfSTED training. Heads felt that having a trained inspector on the staff gave the school a distinct advantage.

Schools reported using the inspection handbook for development planning, staff development, monitoring teaching quality, school self-evaluation ('self-inspection') and governor training. Primary heads' responses to questions about the OfSTED Framework demonstrated that most recognised its importance in the life of the school as well as its vital function in guiding the school's preparations for inspection. The relationship between perceptions of the importance of the Inspection Framework and the outcomes of inspection demonstrated that there was no relationship between heads' interest in the handbook and inspection judgements. There was, however, a tendency for heads who showed little or no interest in the handbook to be more disappointed with the results of their inspection. Headteachers who emphasised the importance of the OfSTED criteria *before* the inspection were more optimistic about the school's prospects for improvement when the inspection had been completed. This was particularly noticeable when heads who had relied heavily on their copy of the handbook were asked about the school's prospects for improvement in twelve months' time.

Accounting for success

When primary heads who were pleased with their inspection were asked to say why they believed they had received a good report, the most common suggestions were about the documents which the school used to support its case. It was clear that many primary heads had decided that co-ordinators should be armed with files or 'portfolios' of photographic and other evidence designed to demonstrate the quality and diversity of the curriculum. This was often felt to have been a good decision with beneficial effects on the outcomes of the inspection. Those few heads who felt that inspection preparations had not been effective made suggestions which seemed to be more obviously related to standards, the quality of teaching and other matters which are of central importance in the OfSTED Framework. Their views had usually been formed as a result of an inspection that had not gone as well as had been hoped.

The effects of the preparation phase on school development are complex and as teachers' accounts of their preparations have shown, it cannot be concluded that the announcement of a forthcoming inspection usually helps schools to improve. For the 10 per cent of heads who come to realise that preparations were not effective, the experience may prove helpful in enabling them to focus on the quality of education which their schools provide, improving the standards achieved by their pupils, the efficient management of schools and the spiritual, moral, social and cultural development of pupils. These are the statutory bases for inspection and a rational planning process to achieve improvements in these areas is at the heart of the OfSTED approach. Heads' and teachers' approach to pre-inspection preparation and their apprehension about the possible consequences of a poor inspection report have diminished inspection's effectiveness. As a result, inspection preparation in many primary and secondary schools concentrated on presenting existing practice in the best possible light. As a primary school deputy head remarked: 'They say inspection is a snapshot. But when you have your wedding photographs done you don't sit there in your ordinary clothes do you?'

Activity in the preparation period saps time and nervous energy that might otherwise have been used to teach and assess pupils or bring about improvements to the school. From an external perspective, teachers' hectic preparations may seem on occasions, even to the teachers themselves, to be a waste of time. But which of us placed in the situation of teachers in the pre-inspection period would not go to extraordinary lengths to avoid loss of confidence and professional credibility? How many, in the midst of such energy and emotion, would think critically and take a more measured approach?

The events of the pre-inspection preparation period are a logical and a predictable response but cannot be lightly dismissed. They have probably been enacted to some degree in a very large proportion of all the 23,500 or so state funded schools in England and Wales and the cost to schools can be considerable. An OfSTIN commissioned study (Brunel University CEPPP and Helix Consulting, 1999) estimated the costs of an inspection to a median sized primary school as £11,500 and to a secondary school as £40,000. Precise costings are not available but these OfSTIN estimates suggest that the cost of the preparation period for every school probably needs to be calculated in thousands rather than hundreds of pounds.

More serious, perhaps, is the effect on pupils' learning. Cullingford and Daniels (1999), in a study that has been heavily criticised by OfSTED, found that pupils are more likely to achieve five or more GCSEs in years in which their school was not being inspected by OfSTED. They also noted, as a result of their analysis of the results of over 47,000 pupils, that inspections carried out between March and June (the examination period) had particularly adverse effects on pupils' GCSE results. It might be argued that the financial cost to schools is fully justified if the implementation of the post-OfSTED action plan brings about significant improvements to the school and has the effect of raising educational standards in schools generally. This study, however, has the worrying implication that the price for any improvements that can be detected is often a reduction in the quality of education for pupils who are unlucky enough to be in the school when their teachers are preoccupied with pre-inspection preparations. OfSTED have dismissed these findings and have claimed that there is no significant relationship between inspection and examination results (*TES*, 23 October 1998). It is possible, however, that research of this kind has played a part in influencing OfSTED's decision to reduce the period of notice before an inspection to 8–12 weeks and thus reduce the disruption experienced by schools in the pre-inspection period.

School improvement: the opportunity costs

Teachers' time and energies are expended in a number of ways. Firstly, they are taken up by the 'daily round' in school and its attendant pressures from pupils, parents, colleagues and the head. Secondly, there are clerical and administrative tasks, lesson and curriculum planning processes, recording, assessment and marking activities and the endless search for appropriate resources and new ideas to provide inspiration and fuel classroom activity. These might be seen as the 'maintenance tasks' that keep the teaching programme running effectively. Thirdly, there is the agenda of development and improvement in which teachers join with colleagues in discussing school-wide policies and practices which need to be understood by everyone in 'the teaching team'. Fourthly, there are the externally imposed demands which include national priorities that require the school to comply with amended regulations, curriculum changes and new content for or approaches to the teaching of particular subjects (e.g. the national literacy strategy (DfEE, 1998a)). Preparing for OfSTED inspection and implementing post-OfSTED action plans are a fifth set of requirements which, at particular moments, can exert considerable, additional pressures.

Although writing in North America about school improvement, Fullan (1991) reminds us that schools are often wary of the implications of any proposed changes. Teachers have little time for renewal or development and need to preserve stability and conserve the time and emotional energy needed to cope with the daily round. This suggests that the activity in the pre-inspection period has other costs that are difficult to measure but are, nevertheless, likely to be significant. The energy committed to the pre-inspection period comes from a limited additional supply that is not easily renewed. It is important, therefore, to ensure that it is used to advantage and that decisions to expend that supply are carefully considered. The impression gained from our study of the pre-inspection period in schools was that teachers' hard work was not carefully co-ordinated or accurately targeted at improving the school because heads and teachers needed to give priority to defending themselves against the damaging consequences of a critical inspection report.

It may be that, when schools are reinspected, they will not suffer from this disadvantage. The results of our study of reinspections in nine secondary schools are discussed in Chapter 6 which reports that schools felt better prepared, put less effort into their preparations and were keen to ensure that their existing plans were not diverted by OfSTED preparation. It may be that primary schools will also be more relaxed 'the second time around'. However, it may not always be possible to convince staff that they are bound to find a reinspection to be a pleasanter and a less burdensome experience.

Professional issues for discussion

- How can schools make best use of external consultants in the run-up to inspection?
- Can heads ensure that the pre-inspection period does not hinder school-wide improvements?
- What is the best way of using the large amount of energy devoted to preparation?

4

The week of the inspection

The provisions for inspection were set out in the Education (Schools) Act of 1992 and are described in Circular 7/93. The minimum length of an inspection is always indicated in the contract and while, typically, 'inspection week' might last for three or four days, its length depends on the size of the school and its particular circumstances. If it is deemed necessary to extend the length of the inspection beyond the contracted minimum, that is a matter for the registered inspector (RgI) because as soon as a contract has been granted the RgI, and not OfSTED, is responsible for the conduct of the inspection. The inspection team must report on the quality of education provided (teaching, curriculum, assessment, pastoral care and relationships with parents), educational standards (pupils' attainments, progress, attitudes to learning, behaviour and attendance), leadership, and the efficient management of financial and other resources. Finally, the spiritual, moral, social and cultural development of pupils is assessed by looking at what the school does to promote the understanding of right and wrong, teach pupils about religious and cultural diversity and foster a sense of responsibility towards others in school and in the community.

These matters are not judged solely on the basis of observations and interviews during inspection week but also as a result of the study of documents and other information provided by the school. These would include the prospectus, reports to parents, the governors' annual report, the school development plan, curriculum plans, schemes of work, policy documents, registers, and samples of pupils' work from every class in the school. Before an inspection takes place, the school will also have been asked to invite the parents to a meeting with the registered inspector which provides them with an opportunity to communicate their opinions directly. Parents are also asked to complete a questionnaire which seeks their opinions about the school. Inspection reports do not report the views of parents unless they are supported by other evidence collected during the course of the inspection. In addition, the headteacher is required to complete the 'Headteacher's Form' and provide a written statement about the school and its aims. Inspectors are provided with detailed information from OfSTED about the school's results in national tests and data which allows them to make comparisons with national averages and the performance of other schools in the locality. The imposing sounding 'Pre-inspection Context and School Indicator' form, the PICSI, which is sent by OfSTED to the RgI, provides comparative data for similar schools. The PICSI, if available, is taken to the school by the RgI on the pre-inspection visit, discussed with the head and, if necessary, updated in the light of new evidence about the school. Comparative performance and assessment data (PANDAs) have recently been made available to all schools annually to assist with planning and target-setting.

There is a great deal of paperwork and some official concern about its potentially disruptive effect on pupils' education. Schools feel that they must produce new documents for the inspectors and review, revise and update their policy documents and curriculum plans in readiness for the inspection. This can create a large additional burden for schools and the need to produce these documents can have a major impact on the workload of the head and senior members of staff. The nursery and primary handbook issues a stern warning to inspectors who may feel tempted to demand even more paperwork from the schools and gives some advice to schools which might seem (to headteachers who feel they have no choice in the matter) to be unrealistic and insincere:

> It is important that schools do not feel that substantial documentation must be produced specially for the inspection. Some additional items, for example, attendance registers, samples of pupils' records and reports to parents, may be required by inspectors during the week of the inspection, often to be used in conjunction with the samples of pupils' work. On no account should inspectors issue additional forms to the school for completion, beyond those prescribed by OfSTED (OfSTED, 1995, p.20).

During 'inspection week', the lead inspector and inspection team members observe teaching, interview teachers, discuss the management of the school with the head and governors, scrutinise records, look at pupils' work, assess the appropriateness of resources and report on the spiritual, moral, social and cultural development of pupils at the school. The analysis of the data provided by the head, the results of National Curriculum tests and public examinations, and the impressions gained from the study of the paperwork are all taken into account before judgements are made.

Early contacts

Our pre-inspection survey of primary heads (whose schools were about to be inspected in the summer of 1998) explored their experiences of contacts with the lead inspector or RgI in the period before the inspection began. When we looked at primary schools in mid-April 1998 that were due to be inspected in May (i.e. in the next three- to six-week period) it was discovered that over 85 per cent of them had received at least one visit from their RgI and one in three had been visited more than once. However, 13 per cent of schools were yet to receive their first visit, although in every case, initial contacts with these schools had been made in other ways (by letter and telephone). Very few heads (4 per cent) reported that they had been made more anxious by these early contacts and most had found the RgI's visit provided reassurance and helpful information. Even the heads of schools that had not yet been visited had found their early contacts with their RgI to be 'reassuring'.

This seems to suggest that all registered inspectors should follow normal practice and make an early visit to schools and provide information about the inspection. Some clear guidance from OfSTED to contractors, RgIs and schools would be useful in clarifying expectations. If the school's inspection preparations are not meeting requirements, and this advice is given too late or not at all, the school is disadvantaged. It is likely that the detailed discussions that can take place during an early face-to-face visit would make it more likely that RgIs would identify problems and give heads clearer guidance about the requirements of the forthcoming inspection. A first visit just a week or two before the inspection may disadvantage the school if it does not provide sufficient time for the head, staff and governors to consider and act upon any advice that might be given.

Managing the inspectors

So how should the head and staff respond when inspection week arrives and the inspection begins? Should they fuss about the arrangements for tea and coffee, smile anxious smiles, offer to be as helpful as possible and try not to get in the way? Is the school's aim to be as amenable as possible and allow the inspectors to get on with their job unhindered? There is naturally a sense of anxious expectation as staff begin the week that some teachers described as 'the most important in their professional career'. Should headteachers, in particular, consider how they might manage the inspection? Should the staff discuss the kind of relationships with inspectors that would be most likely to benefit the school?

In the Spring of 1999 we invited two senior staff from OfSTED to a seminar that was attended by the heads of our case study primary schools. Some headteachers took the opportunity to criticise the competence or conduct of one or more members of their inspection team and to tell OfSTED about their misgivings. A member of OfSTED responded with the suggestion that heads should learn to be 'more steely'. It is good advice even if it did come from a surprising source. 'Steeliness' suggests toughness, a willingness to negotiate, the confidence to raise concerns and agree a set of arrangements with the RgI and members of the inspection team that will be helpful to the school. Reasonable requests for information on the progress of the inspection ought not to be resisted and RgIs should not be surprised to be welcomed by confident professionals who wish to present themselves as partners in a school improvement enterprise. A confident, optimistic head can help to solve problems, protect staff from unreasonable demands and ensure that the school keeps the inspectors well informed. It may also help to redress the uneven power differentials (Brimblecombe, Ormston and Shaw, 1996) establish a more equal and a more purposeful relationship and prevent staff from behaving like examination candidates or the defendants in a trial. Pike (1999), for example, points out that it is important to plan for debriefings, establish a timetable, prepare staff for their individual feedback session and maintain what he calls 'a positive mental attitude' (p.57). He suggests, however, that heads need to be ready to counter judgements which they do not believe and correct inaccuracies:

> Where there might be confusion concerning a hypothesis that has been raised or a teaching evaluation that might have been made, it is helpful for the head of department to come to the briefing armed with the concerns and ready to raise them in professional debate with the reporting inspector (p.92).

'Steeliness' in this example is displayed by a readiness to raise concerns, to ask for the evidence on which the judgement is based, arrange discussions, make the case with the support of appropriate evidence and insist that the appropriate subject leader is involved. Our case study interviews asked primary heads whether they felt they had 'managed' the inspection, but this was not a matter that heads had given much attention to and most simply described the ways in which they had tried to maintain high morale and provide reassurance for staff. Few had made conscious efforts to manage the inspectors and hinted that thoughts of managing the inspection seemed too negative and defensive for their taste. They did not see themselves and their inspection team as equal partners in a professional process but as the nervous hosts of important visitors.

> I think I was naïve in this respect. I don't think I thought about managing the inspectors. I wanted to treat them well, make sure they had a nice room . . .

> I made sure they found us enjoyable to inspect. There was a very easy relationship between us all. We were not defensive. This inspection was the reality which we needed to face up to.

The fact that some heads cease to play the part of experienced professionals and place themselves in a subordinate role is understandable. Submissiveness is safe. A normally confident professional might worry that assertiveness, a justifiable complaint about the conduct of the inspection or even the expression of firmly held views about education could place the outcome in jeopardy. Schools are only too well aware of the suggestion that 'the relationship between inspectors and school staff is the most important factor in the success of the inspection' (House of Commons, 1999a, p.35, paragraph 102) and that they and members of their inspection team must both work hard to reduce the risk of disagreement or the possibility of conflict between head and RgI.

Some inspectors unwisely and unfairly make special efforts to ensure that heads are placed in a subservient position. Two of the case study primary schools revealed some examples of what were arguably coded messages intended to remind heads and staff of the power relationship. Several examples came from the same registered inspector in a rural primary school. The head reported, for example, that the RgI put her head round the door of her room and just said the one word 'Bullying?' The surprised headteacher thought for a moment and replied, 'I don't think we have any of that.' The RgI responded, 'Well, I shall decide', before disappearing from the doorway as suddenly as she had arrived. A small number of inspectors may need to be reminded by OfSTED about their responsibilities to maintain appropriate relationships with school staff.

Take us as you find us?

Ball (1997), describing OfSTED's influence on a secondary school, commented: 'What is important here are appearances: having policies for, being seen to, making sure the figures look good.' Hargreaves (1995) noted that schools hide their weaknesses and commented: 'Only the naive do nothing in the run-up to an inspection and adopt a take-us-as-you-find-us approach. In the same way, inspectors assume there is an element of front to be penetrated. The game is understood by both parties' (p.120).

Just over four in ten primary heads claimed that classroom teaching during inspection week was 'typical' or 'fairly typical' of a normal week in the school and a similar proportion (45 per cent) suggested that their schools had put on a highly prepared performance. However, the views of heads who claimed that the teaching in inspection week was not very different, were difficult to reconcile with the views of teachers (see Chapter 3) and the extraordinary lengths to which they went to prepare their lessons for the week of the inspection. In secondary schools 'dull teaching' was often explained away by claiming that the pressures of inspection week had encouraged staff to 'play safe' and concentrate on traditional methods. The 'snapshot' nature of inspection was disliked and secondary school teachers in particular felt that it was unfair for their work to be judged after an observation of 20 minutes or so. These feelings were shared by some primary staff but the views of teachers in secondary schools were probably coloured by the fact that they were normally observed on only two or three occasions in marked contrast to many primary staff who had inspectors in their classroom for a much larger proportion of the lessons that they taught. However, since our primary school data were collected, OfSTED has issued instructions to inspectors suggesting that teachers should not be observed for more than half of any teaching day (OfSTED, 1998d, p.68).

Tell the whole truth?

Heads were asked whether they found they could speak openly to the registered inspector without fear of undesirable repercussions. Sixty per cent of primary and 68 per cent of secondary heads felt that they were able to talk openly with the RgI. The case study interviews, however, revealed that not all heads were entirely happy with the tactics which had been adopted during inspection week. Some felt that there was no point in trying to hide weaknesses because the inspectors were almost certain to penetrate any disguise. 'Things were drawn to their attention because there was no way they could be disguised' (inner-city primary head). However, heads must balance the risks of being caught out, appearing not to know what is happening in their school – 'I wanted them to know that I knew what was what . . . and that we were realistic and honest' (head of a rural primary school) – with revealing so much to the inspectors that the report became more critical than it might otherwise have been. It was not always easy to get the balance quite right and the head of the rural school who decided to be open and honest reflected on her decision and seemed to regret it:

> I told them about the school's weaknesses and I think I did the wrong thing. I regretted doing it. They latched on to the school's weaknesses and came in with a very negative approach. I thought I would save time by saying this is what we do well and I also like to give an honest answer so I told them what we needed to pull up on. I heard very little about what we do well but I heard an awful lot about the other things (head of a rural primary school).

The fact that we found heads who felt that they had got the tactics wrong or had not played the game as effectively as they had hoped has important implications and suggests to us that there is a need to allow inspectors and school staff to perceive themselves as working together for school improvement. It is a theme to which we will return.

Heads of schools with 'good' inspection reports were more confident that their strategy had been the right one, but, as with their approach to classroom teaching, there was little agreement about which strategy was correct:

> I was not alerted to any weaknesses that I was not aware of and I did not raise any weaknesses with them. I don't think I should have done. If I take a child from another school, I would need to be told facts but I would not want to be told things that might colour my judgement (headteacher, inner-city primary school).

> When they asked about strengths and weaknesses, it was no problem. I felt, as a head, that I *should* know them. There was no problem in sharing the school's strengths and weaknesses with the registered inspector (headteacher, urban primary school).

Few secondary heads were keen to 'bare all' to inspectors because they felt their interest lay in having as few key issues (KIs) as possible. They perceived KIs as unwelcome criticisms and felt that having too many of them might lead to some loss of support from the school community. Chapter 6 explores further the wide variation in headteachers' stance to openness and honesty during the inspection week and suggests that a change in the approach of inspection teams is timely.

Our research into inspection week in secondary schools discovered that one in five heads ensured that the inspectors were made aware of the school's weaknesses and, as in primary schools, some heads had reasons to regret their decision:

> If I was OfSTEDed again, I wouldn't give away so much information. I'd sit back and say, if you want to find anything out you can jolly well find it out (head of a secondary school).

About a half of the secondary school respondents complained that one or two issues were picked up by the inspectors because the school had drawn attention to them. This complaint about the effects of professional discussions with the RgI during inspection week is strangely contradictory. Did schools really expect to receive some kind of immunity from criticism because the head was first to mention the weakness? Is the inspection team's function to provide only insights and recommendations for development that the staff and governors might not have thought of for themselves? The finding that heads often complained when inspectors acted on their advice deserves attention because it seems to be at the heart of an important weakness in the nature of the system of OfSTED inspection. If inspection was only about public accountability, then the identification of weaknesses would be akin to a confession of guilt. Inspection, of course, is about *both* accountability and improvement and there appears to be a tacit assumption that these dual intentions are necessarily compatible. It is perhaps not surprising that heads who thought only about school improvement were upset when information they had disclosed to the inspectors about the school's weaknesses seemed to be used against them. The House of Common's Select Committee, however, did not see this as a problem and in its report on the work of OfSTED confidently announced:

> We do not agree that the debate on inspection should be based on the supposed dichotomy between 'audit' and 'advice'. This is not an either/or situation (House of Commons, 1999a, paragraph 98, p.34).

While we might agree that the debate should not be based on the dichotomy (see Chapter 2), we are, nevertheless, convinced that it is an important consideration that cannot so easily be dismissed.

If the OfSTED inspection became a less threatening experience and more concerned with school improvement, then inspection might be perceived as a service to schools which most heads would welcome. Free from the risk of public censure, heads and governing bodies might want to abandon costly pre-inspection reviews and elaborate preparations and, rather than 'light touch' inspections, would be likely to demand as thorough an inspection as could be afforded. It is in this climate that schools would be more willing to provide 'warts and all' evidence of their own, apply rigour to systematic 'self-inspection' and be less likely to see the process as a contest or believe that the inspectors are 'cheating' when they score points using ammunition that the school has itself provided. The next chapter explores some of the reasons why matters that concern heads are *not* frequently picked up and given high priority by the inspectors. If change processes are to be encouraged by inspection, there is a need for a multi-level perspective which Hopkins, West and Ainscow (1996) describe as being 'embedded' in an educational system that has to work collaboratively:

> This meant that the roles of teachers, heads, governors, parents, support people (advisers, higher education consultants) and local authorities needed to be defined, harnessed and committed to the process of improvement.

Hopkins *et al.* might well have added OfSTED inspectors to this list. Inspectors have now such an influential position within the system that the outcomes of inspection are arguably a key contribution that needs to be more obviously targeted at school improvement.

Are inspections getting easier?

The 1998 sample of primary heads was noticeably more positive about inspection week and this seemed to suggest that school inspections at the end of the primary school inspection cycle were being conducted in a more positive atmosphere than those carried out at the time of our earlier survey.

Many interviewees in our sample of nine secondary schools that had been reinspected also reported that the inspectors were more competent than in 1993. In general the quality of the inspection was perceived as better; it was widely felt that the poorest inspectors had dropped out and that most teams had members with considerable experience. This had resulted in more thorough inspections and the confidence they engendered led to more worthwhile, informal discussions between inspectors and teachers. As in 1993, however, there were inspectors whose ability was questioned: issues included inspectors' lack of attention to their work, inappropriate behaviour and lack of empathy with the school. Overall, 43 per cent of the interviewees in reinspected schools thought the inspectors 'were professional' and 34 per cent said they were not. The main reasons given for negative judgements about inspectors were that they had poor rapport with the staff, were too old and out of touch, were naïve in their judgements, lacked the required specialisms, were out of sympathy with the school's ethos, or came with a preset agenda. There were no differences here in the views held by teachers at different levels of seniority, but marked differences between schools. Several were concerned that their inspections were rushed, with little time for professional discussion between the head and the RgI.

The outcomes of inspection in primary schools were investigated and seemed to be more favourable in the summer of 1998 than in the spring of 1997. The heads who were surveyed in 1997 included 58 per cent who felt that the inspectors' overall judgement had been that the school was 'good' or 'very good' but the corresponding total for the 1998 cohort was 68 per cent. Both groups of heads were asked whether they felt encouraged by the inspection report and there were many more dispirited heads as a result of the 1997 inspections and fewer who were encouraged by the outcome of their inspection.

Table 4.1 shows that more than twice as many heads felt dispirited by the earlier round of inspections than those who were inspected in the summer of 1998.

Table 4.1 Heads' reactions to the inspectors' judgements

	1 dispirited	2	3 neutral	4	5 encouraged
Survey A 1997	21%	11%	10%	26%	32%
Survey B2 1998	9%	13%	9%	26%	43%

Survey A: N = 374; missing data = 7. Survey B2: N = 311; missing data = 3.

Both of the survey samples of primary school heads were selected at random, but it is possible that the difference can be accounted for by sampling error or the effect of measuring reactions one year after inspection and three to six months after inspection. There was also a possibility that the schools which were left to the end of the inspection cycle were not representative of schools in general. However, both samples contained around 14 per cent of inner-city schools and the average percentage of pupil entitlement to free school meals in each sample was very similar (23 per cent in the 1997 survey and 22 per cent in 1998). There is no evidence that OfSTED had selected schools for the final phase of inspection according to particular criteria and it is unlikely that, with the passage of time, schools take a less favourable view of the outcome of their inspection.

In his fifth annual report, HMCI notes that 'The proportion of schools that fail their inspections remains, however, much the same as in previous years' but begins his report by noting that:

> In 1993/94 the quality of teaching was judged to be less than satisfactory in 25 per cent and 30 per cent of lessons in Key Stages 1 and 2 . . . This year the comparable figures have fallen to 8 per cent . . . (for both key stages). Teaching is now deemed to be good in over half of the lessons observed (OfSTED, 1999b).

Heads' reactions to their inspection and their perception of the inspectors' overall judgement of the school seem to confirm either that inspectors have become gentler and more inclined to recognise strengths in primary schools or, as HMCI suggests, that the quality of teaching is improving.

It is certainly true that the education press has publicised those cases in which RgIs or members of inspection teams seem to have made unduly harsh judgements. The most critical comments have been reserved for those who have allegedly created unhappiness and a loss of confidence in schools. One lead inspector was de-registered in November 1998 following accusations that he had intimidated the staff of several primary schools and caused the head of a school in London to suffer a nervous breakdown. His is now a celebrated case and a reminder to all inspectors to avoid the temptation to indulge in the kind of power-play and posturing that is calculated to make inspections unnecessarily negative and demoralising. If inspectors have become more skilled in building good relationships with schools, friendlier and more likely to make positive points in inspection reports, this seems to suggest that a more relaxed phase in inspection is already heralding the introduction of 'light touch' inspections. Our evidence shows that relationships between inspectors and school staff were generally good and that most heads recognised their RgI's 'professionalism' and 'sensitivity'.

Relationships with the registered inspector

Primary school heads usually express support for the RgI who led their inspection team and this appears to be an encouraging sign and further evidence of inspection's changing culture. It is not that heads had simply failed to penetrate the inspectors' professional front or detect their concealed agendas because our survey of RgIs showed very clearly the extent to which inspectors identify with the schools. Registered inspectors want to do much more than the system currently allows to support schools' efforts to develop and improve. Evans and Penney (1994), writing about the inspectors' inability to advise schools, concluded over five years ago that 'OfSTED's discourse celebrates "disinterest" and "neutrality"' but that was not the stance adopted by inspectors in the current research. Inspectors were keen, within the limitations imposed upon them, to be more involved with schools and their perceptions of their relationship with heads confirmed that it had been a good one. OfSTED may well argue that inspectors are free agents and that schools are able to employ them as consultants after the inspection has been completed. There are some examples where this has happened (Close, 1998). We met with the head of one primary school that had maintained contact with its lead inspector and it was clear that the school was very pleased with the high quality advice and support that it received. However, the opportunity to use the RgI as a consultant is not the same as making provision within the inspection system for inspectors to follow-up the schools they have inspected and offer advice about the implementation of their action plans. Schools may not know that this is a possibility, inspectors may be unwilling or unable to offer support, and RgIs and team members are discouraged from offering their services to schools (see Chapter 8).

The extent to which good relationships with inspectors depended on the outcome of the inspection was investigated. Ten of the twenty primary schools with 'poor'/'very poor' inspection reports commented that their relationship with the RgI had been a 'harmonious' one. Not surprisingly, perhaps, none of the schools with 'very good' reports and only a tiny minority of those with 'good' reports (less than 3 per cent) noted that their relationship with their RgI was not a good one. Heads and registered inspectors, it seems, were able to maintain good relationships whether the outcome of the inspection was favourable or not.

Heads' comments often praised the lead inspectors for their professionalism and sympathetic approach.

> We were fortunate to have an inspector who wanted to support the school.
>
> I got on very well with the RgI. We seemed to speak the same language.
>
> We agreed on everything. I had complete faith in them. They were a pleasure to have in the school.
>
> I thoroughly respected her as a professional with integrity.

There were more than 20 expressions of the belief that 'we were lucky' from heads who believed that the fortunate intervention of an exceptionally good inspection team allowed them to escape the worst effects of inspection.

> They were a team that came looking for positive things as well as weaknesses. We had heard horror stories from other schools.
>
> The team were extremely thorough, professional and courteous. I had spoken with colleagues who had not had such a favourable experience.

Feedback on teaching quality

During 'inspection week', the inspectors observe teaching and make judgements about the quality of every lesson that they have observed. At the end of the week, feedback on the outcomes of the inspection is given to the headteacher (sometimes accompanied by the chair of governors) in a verbal report. The RgI often makes arrangements to relay the findings to the full governing body at a later date if the governors are not available on the day the inspection ends. Grades and individual feedback on teaching quality are now given to every teacher who has been observed and heads, but not governing bodies, receive reports on all teaching staff. The full written report – which will not include information on individual teachers – has to be sent to schools no more than five weeks after the inspection has been completed (OfSTED, 1996, p.9).

In 1997, inspectors did not routinely provide feedback for the teaching staff that they had observed and, as the case studies revealed, this was generally seen as a disappointing omission. It caused confusion and resentment from staff who felt that the lack of detailed feedback put them at risk of being blamed for failures for which they were not responsible. As one teacher in an inner-city school noted, 'I felt that my teaching was very good and I was being tarred with the same brush'. For others the lack of feedback (in 1997) caused confusion and some agonising about who precisely had been responsible for any poor quality teaching which the inspectors had observed:

> There was no feedback on my teaching and I have not changed my classroom practice. I wondered if it was me who was responsible for poor teaching. It may have been me. I did not change anything because I did not know what to change. All I did know was that certain members of Key Stage 2 had been picked up on teaching but I still have no knowledge if it was me. All of me? Some of me? The head had no information (maths co-ordinator in a primary school).

Other staff remembered just a brief comment or a few words of encouragement:

> Feedback on teaching? As one inspector walked through my room he said, 'That was very nice' (English co-ordinator urban school).

> There was very little feedback and it was very general. One inspector said 'It was fine. Don't worry!' (deputy head urban school).

This was not thought to be a satisfactory situation and some staff felt that they had been ignored.

> The report at the end tells you about the school but, as an individual teacher, you don't get anything out of it. My teaching style is not the result of OfSTED (English co-ordinator inner-city school).

> They come in. They watch you. They make their decision. The whole point is to help us to improve but if you don't actually get to talk to one or explain things or ask things then it's hard to see how it can improve you (deputy head rural school).

Teachers' comments from the case studies of the 1997 inspection cohort left little doubt that individual feedback to teachers was an important missing element in the arrangements for inspection. Between April 1996 and July 1997, the system did require RgIs to give verbal feedback to heads on the performance of particularly good and particularly poor teachers. Our research into secondary heads' perceptions of the usefulness of this feedback (Fidler *et al.*, 1998) discovered widespread discrepancies between inspectors' gradings and schools' own judgements. The finding raises questions about the potentially significant effects on individual teachers of judgements that may lack validity because they may be made on the basis of too few observations or data that are unreliable for a variety of other reasons.

In September 1997, the system was revised and extended further and by the summer term 1998, feedback to teachers had become a routine part of every inspection. The case study teachers were pleased to receive feedback but, when interviewed, gave the impression that the feedback was usually insubstantial and failed to meet their expectations.

You were given an individual interview about your teaching and the grades were given to you directly. I was very pleased with the feedback. I got (grade) 'twos' and she made suggestions about how I could get 'ones'. It has not altered my practice. The tips given were to check the understanding of children with learning difficulties, buy books and go on a co-ordinator's course. As a classroom teacher, the only useful advice was about registers. It was a key issue (English co-ordinator rural school).

The feedback was not really useful. It was mostly to do with English co-ordination. There was not much on classroom teaching. Nothing particular to change, except outdoor play things which we now have – so that's changed (English co-ordinator inner-city school).

The only negative thing was something I told them myself. I did not have time to mark books. In the end the RgI came back and said this one issue needs to be worked on. I don't know whether they would have raised the issue if I had not raised it. They had had my books for a couple of days and no one came to me to say they hadn't seen work marked (maths co-ordinator in the same inner-city school).

I got feedback for every session. If they did not tell me at the end of the session, they would come and find me. I think I have become more focused on my teaching. There was nothing specific. Nothing major (English co-ordinator rural school).

Registered inspectors' views on feedback to teachers was also sought and the RgIs were asked, 'In your view, is the policy of giving feedback working well?' Almost one-half of the registered inspectors agreed that the system for providing teacher feedback was working well, over one-third had reservations and one in ten did not agree that it was working well. Many of the comments emphasised the difficulty inspectors had of providing effective feedback in the limited time available. There was insufficient time to analyse and prepare feedback before the end of the inspection week. One RgI, for example, remarked on the difficulties of discussions about 'the complexities of the teaching/learning process' in the limited time available 'between lessons'. Some noted that what might be seen as one of the major benefits from an inspection was proving to be a missed opportunity:

It could be better with more time after the inspection is over for more intensive dialogue in a more relaxed setting.

Feedback is technical and requires skill and is very important. To tack it on to the end of an inspection when everybody is tired is not as useful as it could be.

Inspection weeks are intense and busy times for inspectors and the school. Feedback requires detailed planning and the appropriate atmosphere for teachers to gain most from it. This is difficult to achieve during inspection week.

There were also criticisms of the observation and grading forms. As one RgI noted: 'the form stating grade categories is a disaster. Not only does it often demotivate, it is often wrong and leaves inspectors wide open to criticism.'

The compression of teacher grades meant someone on the verge of grade 5s in several lessons receives the same grade as one on the verge of 3s. In other words, there was felt to be insufficient differentiation. Other comments focused on the inability or reluctance of some inspectors to report on unsatisfactory teaching.

Despite the concerns of so many RgIs, feedback sessions were usually appreciated by teachers because they removed the feeling of isolation felt before feedback was introduced. Teachers recognised the limitations of feedback sessions and simply wanted them so that they could hear, at first hand, the grades which their teaching had been awarded. Most of all they wanted to hear that their teaching was good or at least to be assured, as one teacher put it, that they 'hadn't let the side down'. (Registered inspectors noted that some teachers found it very hard to accept adverse criticism no matter how well packaged and presented.) The substance of feedback, however, did not seem to do anything to alleviate the sense of anti-climax which the week of the inspection often brings and few teachers in the case study schools could think of ways in which feedback might have had an influence on their practice.

The end of inspection week

This chapter has noted how important the week of an inspection is in the life of any school and in the professional lives of teachers. It is treated a little like examination finals with all the strain and excitement that they can bring. However, an inspection does not mark an ending of any kind except possibly the stress of the pre-inspection preparation period which teachers occasionally described as being 'worse than the inspection itself'. Despite the perception of inspectors' professionalism and fairness and their normally cordial relationships with staff, the process has casualties. There may be relatively few heads who are disillusioned or angry as a result of their inspection but there are a sufficient number to cause concern. The process leads some heads and teachers to express a determination to do all that they can to avoid a reinspection. The head of a rural primary school felt, despite the good report that his school had received, that the inspection had been a generally negative experience and commented, 'No staff will be here the second time around – myself included.'

A deputy head in an inner-city school in which staff generally had been discouraged by the inspection took comfort from the fact that she did not need to continue in the profession if she no longer enjoyed teaching and added that the inspection 'made a lot of people feel that they would rather not go through another'. Whether these teachers will carry out their threat to move schools or retire to avoid another inspection remains to be seen, particularly as the possibility of 'light touch inspections' had not been announced at the time. Nevertheless, the feelings that prompt such reactions demonstrated that inspection week can be a very unsettling experience for some school staff. Failure and its consequences is, for most schools, very remote but inspection is sufficiently 'high stakes' to create worries which help to explain why teachers find the experience to be stressful and exhausting. The head of an inner-city school that had received a good inspection report explained the difficulty: 'Everybody is scared of being a serious weakness or a special measures school.' Afterwards they (the staff) said, "What are we working for now?" They were completely deflated. It is a very common reaction and one which is discussed in more detail in Chapter 6.

Professional issues for discussion

- Should headteachers and staff manage the inspection? If so, how?
- What kind of relationships with inspectors would be most likely to benefit the school?
- Should heads learn to be 'more steely'?
- 'The relationship between inspectors and school staff is the most important factor in the success of the inspection' (House of Commons, 1999a). How do heads and staff ensure that the relationship is right?
- Teacher feedback requires detailed planning and the appropriate atmosphere for teachers to gain most from it. How can this be achieved during inspection week?

5

Key issues for action: improvement after inspection?

Introduction

The identification of key issues for action (KIs) is a fundamental part of the inspection process. They are the most important outcome of any inspection and, in theory, the main foundation for action to bring about school improvements. Key issues restate the main findings of inspection reports in terms of the actions which, the inspectors believe, are required to remedy any weaknesses that have been identified and to enable the school to 'improve'. They may also refer to areas of strength and may suggest the school continues to maintain high standards in some aspect of their work. In a well-produced inspection report, every key issue will be supported by a variety of evidence and the action required by the KIs will be entirely consistent with that evidence and with the report's main findings. For example, if one of the report's main findings stated that there were problems with pupil behaviour, the key issue for action might require the school to use better behaviour management techniques or simply apply its existing behaviour policy more consistently. After the feedback session on the final day of the inspection, inspectors do not routinely return to explain key issues so a school that does not know how a policy can be implemented more consistently or does not fully understand the phrase 'behaviour management techniques' may find itself in difficulties. (It is in such cases that LEA advisers and consultants can usually be relied upon to provide the advice and support which is needed.)

The registered inspector (RgI) responsible for writing the key issues must, therefore, be satisfied that their meaning is clear. Key issues may require considerable skill in drafting but it is an important investment of the RgI's time because those that are free from ambiguity and confusion are more likely to be influential. Clear, relevant statements not only affect the quality of the action plan that the school's governing body must produce within 40 days of the receipt of the report, but give direction to the school's development or improvement plan (SDP/SIP) into which the action plan is often incorporated. Key issues for action are also included in the inspection summary report that is distributed to parents. Schools also distribute the action plan to parents either in its entirety or, more usually, as a summary of the main points (OfSTED, 1998c).

Characteristics of key issues

The research project provided an opportunity to study a large number of key issues and to note some of their characteristics. Some KIs were complex statements which might have been better expressed as a number of separate issues. Key issues were found which had been expressed as a number of bullet points referring to different National Curriculum subjects and six key issues in some reports might have been better expressed as ten or more in a more logically constructed list. It seems that inspection teams were trying to minimise the number of key issues without actually reducing the range or complexity of the substance of the report on which they required the school to act.

About seven in every ten schools in the sample obtained the services of an LEA consultant or adviser to help them to formulate their action plan and about one in five schools believed that the contribution of LEA advisers had been a major one. The Education (Schools) Act 1992 (see Circular 7/93) decreed that additional resources to fund post-OfSTED action planning should remain in the control of local authorities and an LEA would study the action plan before it released post-OfSTED funding to a school. However, except for schools in special measures or with serious weaknesses (see Chapter 9), feedback or advice on the quality of action planning is not provided by OfSTED or inspection teams unless the school had decided to employ their RgI as a consultant after the inspection was over. Many heads and governors were puzzled by this. As a head and deputy head at one of the case study schools noted:

> I just submitted an action plan and it was not challenged. I just assume it's OK (headteacher).

> We were on tenterhooks wondering if the plan would be accepted (deputy head at the same school).

Most schools interpreted this official silence as consent but had no evidence that their action plan had been read by anyone.

Given the importance of key issues to schools and their essential role in inspection and the school improvement process, they were given an emphasis in our research. One aim was to determine schools' reactions to their KIs and their effect on school development and improvement after the inspection. However, this chapter not only looks at this important general issue but examines some specific questions which emerged during the course of the research. Schools often believed that they had anticipated the outcomes of their inspection and had 'learned nothing new' and this convinced some heads that inspections did not give good value for money. There was also an interest in 'fashions' in key issues and the function of inspection reports in providing an emphasis for particular messages about the shortcomings of the nation's schools. These broad intentions have been expressed as a number of related questions:

- What did schools think of their key issues?
- Were heads convinced of their importance?
- Did the key issues reported by inspectors provide any consistent messages about the common weaknesses to be found in schools?
- Were the key issues that (i) inspectors identified as frequently occurring and (ii) heads predicted would be listed in their inspection reports, the same or different?

The final section of the chapter discusses some implications for practice in schools and for the future development of inspections.

Headteachers and key issues for action

Over 90 per cent of schools involved in our research were given six or fewer key issues, although, as noted previously, the use of complex, multifaceted statements by some inspection teams made the process of counting KIs a fairly pointless one. Heads, however, did not consider this to be a matter for concern and were happy to report the length of their list and state how many key issues they had rated as important.

On average, primary schools were given just over four key issues although we found a wide range from zero to 18. (About two-thirds of schools received either three, four or five KIs.) Generally, heads considered their schools' key issues to be significant ones. About one-quarter of headteachers declared that *all* of their key issues were 'important' or 'very important' and three-quarters of them had faith in the importance of at least half of the key issues listed in their inspection reports.

When heads were asked if their list of key issues contained any which they would find difficult or impossible to progress, around three in ten heads stated that they had been given at least one 'difficult' key issue. This was often seen as difficult because of resource implications or because the issue concerned raising standards or improving teaching quality and both were seen as challenging and essentially long-term enterprises.

Inspection teams did seem capable of providing key issues that most heads perceived as relevant and helpful in providing a sense of direction that met with general approval. However, KIs were usually seen as giving an impetus for matters which were already under review rather than opening up areas for development that the school might not otherwise have considered. There is a growing body of research (Ouston, Earley and Fidler, 1996; Cuckle, Hodgson and Broadhead, 1998) which notes that schools report that they had learned little that was new as a result of their inspection but, as Millett and Johnson (1998a) have reported, the effect of inspection was often to 'add impetus to on-going developments by reinforcing management decisions and strategies' (p.254). Lonsdale and Parsons (1998), in their small-scale study, discovered that, on average, three-quarters of the key issues had been identified by their sample schools before the inspection.

However, all of these studies gathered evidence from interviews and questionnaires which were completed by teachers and, more frequently, by headteachers, *after* the inspection had taken place. It is a finding that was confirmed by our own surveys of heads. For example, when primary heads were asked to indicate on a five-point scale the extent to which their 'action plan was restating developments already in the school development plan', more than half chose the first two categories indicating that 'all' or 'nearly all' of the post-OfSTED action plan was already included. Those who felt that the action plan focused 'entirely' or 'almost entirely' on different areas from the current SDP (the two lowest categories) constituted, in total, only one in twenty (5 per cent) of the sample. When the primary school heads in the follow-up survey were asked if any of the inspectors' decisions had surprised them, six out of ten declared that the inspection held no surprises.

Heads were asked to list their two most important key issues and to state whether they had anticipated that they would be identified by the inspectors. Fifty-seven per cent of heads reported that they had correctly predicted their two most important KIs, exactly one-third had predicted one of them and only 10 per cent had failed to anticipate either correctly. This finding not only confirmed much previous research but matched common-sense conceptions of the inspection process. Heads know their schools well, many talk openly with the RgI and feel they have nothing to hide, and inspectors, prompted in many cases by conversations with heads and teachers, note the shortcomings which school staff have identified. This is what teachers believed and a typical comment was: 'I am convinced that inspection is an expensive process which only tells you what you already know.' However, our research showed that the heads' belief was *not* supported by the evidence.

In the 1998 pre-inspection survey of primary schools, heads had been asked to state the two most important key issues that they believed would appear in their inspection report. In their post-inspection survey, they were asked to write down the two KIs they believed had been the most important and then to say whether they had anticipated either or both of them before the inspection had begun. They were then asked to state the number of their KIs and either to list all the remaining ones or enclose a copy of the KIs from their inspection report.

Headteachers' pre-inspection predictions were compared with the KIs that they believed to be the most important and then with all other KIs. In cases of doubt a very generous interpretation was applied so any mention of a key issue in the same general area was counted as a match and awarded one point. For example, a school that predicted that their provision of information technology and the role of governors would be the most important areas for action but whose KIs were about management, provision for the most able, assessment and the monitoring of teaching would score zero. However, it was quite likely that such a school *would* report that it had anticipated at least one of its two most important key issues. When the heads' predictions were compared in this way with the outcomes of inspection, it was discovered that 43 per cent of headteachers had listed two KIs which could not be found in any form on the list which actually appeared in the inspection report and 46 per cent had correctly identified one key issue. Only one in ten (11 per cent) had listed two issues before the inspection which were both in the final report. The implications of these findings make the future of school self-evaluation seem bleak, but discussion of the possible reasons why heads were not generally successful in predicting their KIs has been postponed to Chapter 11 which looks in more detail at this issue and its implications.

Two case studies of schools with 'very good' inspection reports were helpful in shedding further light on the ways in which schools responded to their key issues. Both of these case study schools had confident heads who expressed a vision and a purpose for their school which, in some senses, relegated the effects of inspection to a second or third division of priorities or, in the case of School B, viewed them as a necessary but unimportant chore. The second head (School B), in particular, made comments that are a very good example of a lack of 'steeliness' (see Chapter 4) or the 'obedience' that is all too understandable given the way in which OfSTED and some inspection team members have interpreted inspection's role.

> It's not the most exciting list of key issues, is it? Apart from the registers (which were done in a day) we have not completed anything else. As a staff we have assessment to look at as a detailed issue the whole of this year and we don't want to get into knee-jerk reactions working on an action plan. We want to see the OfSTED inspection as part of the general auditing of what we are out to install. It informs our development plan (head, School A).

> The report was not terribly relevant. It distracted us from more important matters. About ten days ago we had a staff meeting on citizenship. I was at a headteachers' meeting the next day and I was saying that this adviser was very good on citizenship. I told them (the other heads) that citizenship was one of the key issues from our inspection. Well everybody just fell about laughing and said what are you doing that for? We have to do this by law. We are not about to break the law. Obviously in the next inspection that's the first thing they will be looking for. I have said this to you but I would not let the inspectors know. If you are going to be inspected, you must seem to believe what they say. Just because I don't share their view professionally does not mean to say that we are planning to take on OfSTED (head, School B).

Our surveys of primary and secondary school heads discovered that they often believed that they had 'learned nothing new' from inspection and were convinced that they could predict the key issues which would be published in their inspection reports. When the survey sample of 305 secondary heads were asked (using a six-point scale) how confidently they could predict the outcomes of their school's inspection, 80 per cent chose one of the top two categories of the scale indicating a very high level of confidence. Only 2 per cent chose the bottom two scale points which indicated that they could not confidently predict their key issues. Primary school heads also felt that they could anticipate the inspection's findings and the experience of being inspected did nothing to undermine their belief.

Most frequent key issues

The research aimed to discover which key issues were most frequently included in inspection reports, whether heads knew about the issues which were current and whether there had been changes over the period of the last four years. Earlier research on these questions (Maychell and Pathak, 1997) was impossible to replicate because of the difficulties, encountered in the present research, of counting key issues and deciding how they should be classified. It was also a problem that Russell (1996) discovered in her study of the outcomes of inspection in 22 secondary schools. She noted that 'some inspectors were very precise' but 'sometimes the wording (of the key issues) was more general and open to interpretation'. For example, 'develop the roles and responsibilities of co-ordinators' might mean that they should take responsibility for monitoring the curriculum and the quality of classroom teaching and be more actively involved in the dissemination of good practice in such areas as teaching, assessment and recording.

In the current study, the classification of over 1,200 key issues reported by the heads in the primary school survey was, therefore, a fairly crude process, particularly as most heads chose to list the information in an abbreviated form (e.g. 'co-ordinators' roles' or 'ICT'). The decision to bring together (i) 'co-ordinators' responsibilities' with 'monitoring'; (ii) 'schemes of work' with 'curriculum planning' and (iii) 'senior management team issues' with all references to 'strategic planning and the school development plan' was made because, when detailed information was available, it was clear that the inspectors' use of such phrases was meant to cover very similar areas of activity. The information contained in the tables below is rudimentary but, nevertheless, provides a good indication of the broad areas of interest to the inspectors. The fact that the same information had been collected from more than one source and was remarkably similar strengthens this claim.

In addition to the survey of headteachers, data were collected from a random sample of registered inspectors who were asked to list the two key issues that they most frequently included in their inspection reports. Some RgIs work in both primary and secondary schools but they responded to the survey with reference to primary *or* secondary inspections depending on the

sector in which they had had most experience. The results which are summarised below are of interest for two reasons. First, it is possible to view
them as evidence of the main weaknesses to be found in our schools and as
matters that the chief inspector might want to highlight in his annual report.
However, this would fail to recognise that the OfSTED model of good practice is not the only possible interpretation and that it makes tacit assumptions and holds ideological positions with which others might disagree. A
more critical view, perhaps, is that the frequently occurring KIs are issues
which were, rightly or wrongly, high on inspectors' agendas. In this view,
the common key issues might be expected to be different from those of last
year or the year before and different again from those which might become
popular in a few years' time.

How do fashions change and how do schools keep in touch with the
prevailing climate of opinion and its changing priorities? There may be
particular emphases in inspector training and in the instructions and advice
in *Update*, the magazine which is regularly distributed by OfSTED to all
inspectors. The advice of government, the concerns of the press and the way
they are absorbed into the inspection culture and act as an influence upon
discussions in schools are also important. One view of inspection activity
might therefore prefer to see OfSTED inspectors as a conduit for the kind of
opinions that can be heard on public platforms rather than a source of
eternal truths about the nature of teaching and learning. However, the
simplest explanation for changes in the emphases of key issues is that
schools have improved and that the areas of weakness that attracted attention some years ago are no longer much in evidence because heads, governors and staff have taken the necessary remedial action.

Four sources of information threw light on these questions – three from
our own research and one from elsewhere. The first source of evidence was
the predictions of the 370 primary school sample heads who were asked
about the two most important key issues which they anticipated *before* the
inspection (see Table 5.1). The second source was the key issues that were
actually reported by these same heads after their inspection had been completed (see Table 5.2). The third source was the key issues that registered

Table 5.1 Key issues most frequently predicted by heads

KI predicted	Frequency
Standards	40%
Information technology	31%
Co-ordinators' roles/monitoring	18%
Assessment/recording	17%
Schemes of work/curriculum planning	16%
Teaching quality	9%

Percentages do not total 100 as more than one response could be made.
Heads predicted a total of 672 KIs. Percentages are of heads predicting, N = 352.

inspectors most frequently include in reports (see Tables 5.3). The fourth was a study of post-inspection action planning undertaken by the NFER (Maychell and Pathak, 1997) which classified the key issues from 115 inspection reports that were issued to primary schools in 1995 and 1996 (see Table 5.4) and made it possible, in the current research, to identify KIs which have recently become more frequently included in inspection reports.

The results of all these analyses of key issues revealed a remarkably consistent picture. It was earlier noted that primary school heads were not particularly good at predicting their own most important key issues and frequently identified at least one important KI that did not subsequently

Table 5.2   Key issues most frequently reported by heads

KI predicted	Frequency
Assessment	40%
Co-ordinators' roles/monitoring	37%
Information technology (ICT)	35%
Standards in the core subjects	31%
Teaching quality	25%
SMT issues/leadership/strategic planning	25%

Percentages are based on the number of schools with these KIs in their reports. 304 schools provided information about their key issues.

Table 5.3   Key issues RgIs report as most frequently included in inspection reports

KI predicted	Frequency
Co-ordinators' role/monitoring	43%
Assessment	32%
Information technology (ICT)	25%
Standards	15%
Schemes of work/curriculum planning	14%
Teaching quality	13%

150 of the 165 inspectors made valid responses and listed 285 KIs.

Table 5.4   Key issues most frequently included in inspection reports (from Maychell and Pathak, 1997)

Key issue	Frequency
Schemes of work	35%
Curriculum planning	32%
Teaching quality	31%
Co-ordinators' role	29%
Monitoring SDP and policies	27%
School Development Planning	26%

Percentages are of primary schools. N =115.

appear in the school's inspection report. However, they were often aware of the items that were high on inspectors' agendas and this made it all the more surprising that they were not better at predicting their own KIs.

Key issue 1 – Assessment

Schools, it seems, would have been wise to review and improve their systems for assessment because four in every ten schools had a key issue about assessment listed in their inspection report (see Table 5.2) and about one in six (see Table 5.1) predicted that it would be one of their two most important key issues. Registered inspectors also recognised that it was an area of weakness that was often the subject of key issues and they frequently commented that it was schools' failure to make effective use of assessment in future planning that concerned them most. Almost one-half of the RgIs who identified assessment as one of their two most frequently used KIs made explicit mention of the fact that the connection between assessment and planning was their main concern. Heads of schools that were about to be inspected might have been well advised to gather evidence that the school was using its assessment data in this way. It was no longer sufficient to provide children with a variety of appropriate modes of assessment. Inspection teams were interested in how teachers used assessment information to guide future planning, but all too often, schools (despite headteachers' general awareness of the importance of assessment issues) were unable to demonstrate that they were doing this satisfactorily.

Key issue 2 – Monitoring, evaluation and the role of curriculum co-ordinators

The key issue most frequently listed by RgIs and the second most commonly mentioned by heads was the area of monitoring, particularly the role of subject or curriculum co-ordinators in monitoring the curriculum, standards and the quality of teaching. Although its importance may have been underestimated in heads' pre-inspection predictions (see Table 5.1), it was the third most frequently predicted KI. The research case studies demonstrated that monitoring and evaluation was not an easy issue to tackle and heads' good intentions were all too frequently unfulfilled (see Chapter 11, pp. 139–40).

Key issue 3 – Information technology

ICT or 'information and communications technology' was the second most frequently predicted key issue and the third most commonly occurring KI in the inspection reports of our sample of primary schools. Heads were concerned about their schools' lack of ICT equipment, lack of money to acquire new computers and the lack of confidence and expertise of staff to make appropriate use of ICT in a wide variety of settings. The inspectors agreed that ICT was a major area for development in primary schools. It is an issue which has recently come to the forefront of inspectors' thinking. (The NFER study which was conducted between 1995 and 1996 (see Table 5.4) did not mention ICT among the most frequently identified key issues.)

Guidance from OfSTED (1998d) reminded inspectors that, for a period of two years, the programmes of study for six subjects had been relaxed to give more time for literacy and numeracy. The requirements for English, mathematics, science, information technology and religious education – the core subjects – remained the same. In 1998, heads knew that the new arrangements would emphasise ICT and many recognised that it was a relatively underdeveloped subject in their school. On this evidence, however, religious education might have been predicted to be a priority because the guidance to inspectors has given it the same importance as ICT (OfSTED, 1998d). Religious education was not predicted by heads and they were right not to do so because it was not frequently included as a key issue in inspection reports. Our survey of RgIs did not identify RE as a frequently occurring key issue.

Key issue 4 – Management, leadership and strategic planning

A key issue that just failed to reach the list of the inspectors' six most frequent choices was ranked fifth equal in the KIs that were actually included in inspection reports of the sample schools. It was the issue that has been called 'management, leadership and strategic planning' but it was not predicted by primary heads to be important. It is unusual (but not unknown) to find a key issue that was directly critical of the quality of a head's leadership and there may be a reluctance on the part of headteachers to admit that such criticisms had been made. There were KIs that suggested that attention should be given to the senior management group, its roles, workload, the function of the deputy head and so forth. Other key issues pointed to a lack of attention to strategic or financial planning or merely identified the school's development plan as in need of revision and updating. Perhaps it is understandable that heads were reluctant to admit or did not realise that their ineffective leadership and management or their inability to plan strategically was contributing to the school's difficulties.

Key issue 5 – Provision for able pupils

Provision for able pupils was a key issue that almost one in ten inspectors declared they had frequently included in recent inspection reports and which one in twenty heads identified as one of their two most important key issues. The schools which predicted that provision for the most able would be one of their two most important key issues generally received reports which did *not* include it among their KIs. In many cases the inspectors had a variety of other concerns (standards, management issues, attendance, teaching quality). It may be that the consideration that these schools had obviously given to the needs of able pupils had made its inclusion less likely, but it is also possible that matters which become KIs depend to a considerable extent on the seriousness of other issues that require the school's attention.

'Management, leadership and strategic planning' and 'provision for able pupils' were not yet in a position to challenge the pre-eminence of 'monitoring', 'assessment' or 'ICT'. However, examination of the most popular KIs in 1995/96 (see Table 5.4) supports the notion that there have been changing emphases in key issues. Heads may need to add 'management, leadership and strategic planning' and 'provision for able pupils' to their development plan before their school is reinspected in a few years' time.

Implications for practice and the future of inspections

Our analysis of key issues has shown that heads and inspectors share a view of the priorities for inspection. The two groups had identified the most important areas for development as:

- pupils' learning and its monitoring and assessment
- teaching quality and its monitoring
- information technology and its capacity to influence the curriculum
- the educational standards achieved by schools
- and (for the inspectors) the quality of school management, leadership and planning.

The inspectors' priorities, as expected, were reflecting and anticipating the interim arrangements for the primary curriculum from September 1998 which, for two years, gave schools 'greater flexibility' in the way that they approached the foundation subjects so that more time could be given to literacy and numeracy. There was no relaxation in the requirements for information technology or religious education. Although the requirements for information technology were given a great deal of emphasis in inspectors' judgements (see Table 5.3), the requirements for religious education were not. Religious education, the daily act of collective worship and mentions of schools' provision for the spiritual, moral, social and cultural development of pupils were infrequently cited among the key issues. Heads seemed to sense that these aspects of the curriculum would not often attract attention and were well aware of the inspectors' priorities.

However, heads' predictions and inspectors' commonly chosen key issues could usually be traced to the agenda of national priorities to which schools were expected to react. It is not self-evidently a list of the interventions which are right for most schools. For example, Russell (1996) concluded, as a result of a study of secondary schools, that the frequent inclusion of 'monitoring' as a key issue could not easily be explained by examining the evidence.

> It is likely that this is because formal monitoring is a relatively new process for all schools and that it is believed to be a 'good thing' so, rather like cod-liver oil, can be offered to the ailing and the healthy indiscriminately (p.335).

The broad sweep of the inspection criteria allows inspectors to select from the wide menu available and, from time to time, to change the priorities which underpin the selection of key issues. A degree of unanimity is probably achieved because inspectors, unwittingly and consciously, follow the dictates of an inspection culture which from time to time is powerfully influenced by the politicians and the press. It is not difficult, for example, to imagine the circumstances in which bullying, racism, parenting or entrepreneurial activity might begin to challenge the pre-eminence of those in the 'KI premier league'. Key issues have provided a mechanism to ensure that schools respond to the needs and whims of the society which they serve. However, post-OfSTED action planning may have been a more powerful agent for change if an appropriate follow-up process had ensured that heads and governors were encouraged and supported in its implementation. Schools may manage the writing of their action plan and the implementation of the key issues bureaucratically, enthusiastically, half-heartedly or ignore them almost entirely if they choose to do so. Heads' and governors' desire to be acknowledged for their work on the action plan and the implementation of their key issues provides an opportunity for some further tightening of procedures which could be achieved with a large measure of consent. Reinspections begin by looking at progress since the last inspection but this is a distant event that does not seem likely to fulfil teachers' needs.

> The teachers would love them to come back: not in an inspectorial way but just to see how they are getting on. Nobody checks up. They don't even check to see that you have sent off your action plan. What's the point of doing it then? (headteacher, inner-city primary school).

This is a very common and a very understandable response. It is also an expression of the school's dependence and desire to please a higher authority from whom a few words of approval would be greatly appreciated. This primary head makes it clear that the reason that the school had worked so conscientiously was to please the inspectors. Heads who had been involved in 'self-inspection' and whose monitoring had contributed to the outcomes of their inspection report would be more likely to ask themselves whether their action had borne fruit. In many ways it would be better if schools felt encouraged because they had identified improving trends in the data rather than by words of approval from a visiting RgI. It is an advantage of internal rather than external inspection that ought not to be overlooked.

Implications for school improvement?

The views of heads and inspectors have implications for practice in schools and the future development of inspection and its use as a vehicle for school improvement. Some of these questions have been raised in previous chapters, some need little discussion and others that require further exploration are discussed in the remaining chapters of this book.

If inspections were to be followed up more systematically, many more schools might feel more involved and better supported. Currently, except for schools in special measures or with serious weaknesses, feedback and advice on the quality of action plans is not available from OfSTED or the inspection team. The role of the LEA could, perhaps, be expanded by insisting that it is formally represented as a member of every inspection team. This would help to improve understanding of the resource implications and improve the quality of inspection follow-up. Currently, LEAs study the action plan before post-OfSTED funding for staff training is released. 'Link advisers' are often good at helping schools to understand the implications of a recently completed inspection.

OfSTED's desire to reduce the number of key issues listed in reports to schools has had the unintended consequence of increasing their complexity. Should not KIs be expressed as a number of clearly separate issues even if this meant increasing their number? It is important to ensure that schools and inspectors recognise that the KIs are listed in order of priority and are aware of the implications for action planning.

Our research shows that heads were convinced of the importance of most key issues. The process of summarising main findings in this way and asking schools to plan to implement the action which they imply is a rational and acceptable approach to school improvement. A formal requirement for schools to submit a 'self-inspection' report for discussion with the inspection team would allow the school's management team to explore the differences between their predicted key issues and the outcomes of inspection. More flexible strategies of this kind that involved the school could prove to be valuable in helping schools to improve their skills in self-evaluation, gain confidence in their own judgements and ensure that 'self-inspection' became a continuous activity that ebbed and flowed across the three terms of each school year (see Chapter 12).

Progress in the medium term
Table 5.5 summarises the progress reported by heads in the primary school case studies when a telephone interview was arranged some five terms after the school had been inspected. The table (see column 2) also includes information about the heads' feelings about the prospects for improvement about a year after the inspection, and their verdict on the progress they felt their schools had made after five terms can be found in column 4.

The results in Table 5.5 contain a number of surprises. They seem to demonstrate that, for this small sample of schools, the results of the

Table 5.5 A brief summary of progress with the key issues reported by primary heads

School location	Head's perception of prospects for improvement (initial questionnaire)	Head's report of inspectors' judgement of the school (questionnaire)	Rate of progress reported by head after five terms	Reasons given for incomplete progress	Key comment from head's follow-up interview by telephone
Rural	High	Good	Very poor	School now in a federation with a new 'one day a week' acting head	'I could not even tell you what the key issues were'
Rural	Medium	Satisfactory	Good	Improving pupils' writing is a long-term aim	'It's what we would have done anyway'
Rural	Low	Satisfactory	Satisfactory	No resources to release staff for monitoring. No suitable INSET found for lunchtime supervisors	'If they come next year, we might, with a bit of luck, have got there'
Urban/suburban	High	Very good	Excellent	Completed work on action plan	'We tackled it all but it's on top of what we consider are the priorities for the school'
Urban/suburban	Medium	Satisfactory	Poor	Huge influx of pupils throughout the school	'Last year we had classes of 40. Work on the AP just went by the board'
Urban/suburban	Low	Poor (special measures)	Good	Three-year plan to raise standards is on course	'There is nothing concentrates the mind like a hanging'
Inner city	High	Satisfactory	Very good	Completed work on action plan	'It gives you ammunition, particularly by identifying unsatisfactory teaching'
Inner city	Medium	Good	Very good	High staff turnover	'The inspection has definitely helped'
Inner city	Low	Poor (serious weaknesses)	Very good	Three-year plan is on target	'HMI reassured. We got support from the LEA but OfSTED inspection did us no good at all'

inspection and heads' satisfaction with it are not the determining factors. For example, the two schools judged by inspectors to be poor had heads who were hostile to inspection when they were originally interviewed in the summer of 1998.

> Improvement through inspection! Definitely not. Naming and shaming and the atmosphere that accompanies OfSTED is wrong. And I believed that they were a group who would feed back useful information based on an outside view! My own morale has nose-dived. The staff have not recovered in a year. The better teachers took it most to heart. And the way the report was worded to parents! It's not helpful to crush us (headteacher of an urban school under special measures).

> There was only grudging recognition of improvements and all the hard work we have put into this school. Good teachers in KS2 were disheartened. Staff are demotivated. It's hard to get back on track (headteacher of an inner-city school with serious weaknesses).

Five terms later there is still evidence of the negative effects of inspection, but both schools had received advice and support from their LEAs and HMI, both heads seemed confident and their schools were making good progress.

> Being in special measures has given me a much sharper focus. It has made us very determined that we are going to push the standards up and we are going to achieve the things that are on the action plan. We can see that there is some movement forward now. We have done a lot. We have been very, very busy. We have done loads of paperwork and monitoring reports and firming up on procedures and writing schemes of work. We have an English improvement group meeting after school and a behaviour policy group. There is lots of activity from small working groups. Loads of time being put in but I am not sure that it is having an impact on what is happening in the classroom. That's the bottom line. There is a lot of organisational stuff but the teachers are still trying to pick themselves up from the feeling that they have failed. It's still with them (headteacher of an urban school under special measures).

> We are well on target. The action plan is due to be completed next July. The positive HMI report reassured us we were on the right lines and we have had good support and feedback from our LEA. I feel regardless of what OfSTED might say and the SATS might show, the school is at least seen by the LEA to be an example of good practice. We have hosted a 'Spotlight on Literacy' evening for the LEA. All the local schools were invited and it was a really big morale booster to think that what we were doing here was being held up as an example. The inspection? I'm still jaundiced about it. I just feel sceptical about the overall quality of inspections. It's pot luck really whether you get a good one or a bad one (headteacher of an inner-city school with serious weaknesses).

Progress on action plans

Table 5.5 shows that there were two schools that were making little or no progress and both of their headteachers described the unusual circumstances which, in their view, accounted for the action plan being set aside. One school, for reasons which cannot be fully explained without identifying the school, had unexpectedly received a very large number of new pupils including many with special needs and some from large families whose poverty was compounded by a variety of other problems.

> The action plan has been placed on the back burner and is no longer thought about by me or the staff. There are too many other problems. When they (the inspectors) do come back, we might have completed the action on the key issues but I don't know whether they will have been completed satisfactorily. A lot of our staff are simply coping, almost going from one crisis to another (headteacher urban school).

The second of the case studies that was not making progress was a small rural school without a headteacher. It had an acting head who worked at the school on only one day each week. She explained that no appointment had been made because the local authority was believed to be considering the introduction of 'federations' and believed that:

> The lack of applicants (for the vacant head's post) may reflect the changes that we think are coming. Someone could apply for the job and discover that it no longer exists. As far as the inspection is concerned, things are on hold . . . On one day a week what more can I do? My remit is to look after the week's admin matters (temporary, part-time, acting head of a small rural school).

Most schools, however, had made good progress and, as the survey data have indicated, heads and governors regarded their action plan and its implementation seriously and were able to provide very clear summaries of progress to date.

Case study schools which were in settled communities, had stable staffing, had received a good inspection report and were relatively free from the kinds of problems described above, made good progress in implementing the action plan even when the head attached little importance to the key issues.

> Improvement through inspection? Not in this school. Improvement is coming through a whole range of different initiatives. The inspection, I would say, is no more than a snapshot of our improvement process. You wouldn't say that the inspection was adding anything to an improvement process which was already in hand (head of an urban primary school).

Despite the apparent scepticism, this head of a school with an excellent inspection report had made good progress with an action plan in which he appeared to have little faith.

This evidence seems to suggest that progress will be slow when schools already under pressure (but not classified as having 'serious weaknesses' or in need of 'special measures') encounter unforeseen difficulties. In some ways it could even be said to be an advantage to be put into 'special measures' (and to a lesser extent 'serious weaknesses') because the additional support that then becomes available makes it easier for significant progress to be made.

Professional issues for discussion

- Are the accountability mechanisms for the post-OfSTED action plan sufficiently robust?
- Primary and secondary school heads often believed that they had 'learned nothing new' from inspection and were convinced that they could predict the key issues which would be published in their inspection reports. Is this the case and, if not, what are the implications for self-evaluation?
- Should schools be required to submit a self-inspection report for discussion with the inspection team after the inspection to allow the school's management team to explore the differences between their predicted key issues and the outcomes of inspection?
- Do the report's key issues help 'focus the mind' and what factors help or hinder progress on the action plan?

6

The inspection of schools with new headteachers

Some writers have concluded that the OfSTED inspection process is unnecessarily stressful because it takes too little account of the school's own evaluation of its progress and development and 'diminishes if not denies the professionalism of teachers' (Southworth and Fielding, 1994, p.176). Our research suggests that headteachers who regard themselves as 'new' do not feel threatened by an inspection and are more open to its possibilities as a catalyst for improvement. This chapter reports some differences between the attitudes to inspection of newly appointed and established headteachers and examines their consequences for staff. Its main purpose, in the light of these findings, is to continue to develop our earlier discussions of the role which OfSTED inspections play in helping and hindering schools to develop and improve.

New heads' support for the inspection process

Some teachers and heads leave their post earlier than they might otherwise have anticipated because an inspection has been announced, others are so affected by the experience that they leave soon after the inspection has been completed and it is not unusual for schools that are judged to be 'failing' to experience a change of leadership. Annually, in England and Wales, about 10 per cent of schools experience a change of headteacher. Our survey of primary schools found that over 20 per cent of headteachers had been appointed less than two years before the inspection took place in the spring term of 1997. More than one in ten of the sample had been appointed in the year since the school's inspection. We found a similar situation in secondary schools where 23 per cent of heads had been in post for two years or less.

New headteachers can claim with some justification that any weaknesses which the OfSTED inspection team uncovers should be laid at the door of the previous head and that more time is needed before an assessment of their performance can be reliably made. A secondary head appointed shortly before the inspection commented:

> I was canny enough to realise that OfSTED was a real opportunity for me. I could hold my hands up and say, 'None of this is to do with me.' I didn't approach inspection with dread. It would provide me with an objective management tool (secondary headteacher).

New heads occasionally made comments which were uncomplimentary about what they saw as their predecessor's 'historical lack of leadership' and it is perhaps unsurprising that many were able to give their full support to the process of inspection even when the OfSTED team was critical of their school.

From the sample of primary schools which were inspected in 1997, a group of 78 primary heads who had been in post for two years or less at the time of the inspection and a group of 183 heads who had been in post for five years or more were identified. (Those who had been in post for more than two years but less than five years or who had not taken up their appointment at the time of the inspection were not included in the analysis.) Heads were asked to rate, on a six-point scale, the contributions that (i) the inspectors' verbal feedback and (ii) the written report had made to the school's development. They were also asked (iii) how valuable they believed the whole inspection process had been for school improvement. Mean values for each of these six-point scales were calculated for the group of new and established heads.

The aggregate scores on these three variables may be seen as a measure of heads' belief in the effectiveness of the OfSTED inspection process as a means of encouraging schools to develop and improve. The overall mean score for new headteachers was considerably higher than that of established heads and a statistically significant difference ($p<0.01$) was found between the means of these aggregate 'satisfaction' scores. In fact, a group of 31 new heads, who believed that their schools had been assessed as 'satisfactory' or 'poor', expressed greater faith in inspection as a catalyst for school improvement, than a group of 112 established heads who felt that their schools had been assessed as 'good' or 'excellent'. New headteachers, it seems, were more appreciative of their OfSTED inspection than established heads and this remained true even when the report on their school had *not* been perceived as a good one.

The possibility that factors other than the length of service of the heads may have accounted for the difference was explored. Differences between school type, number of pupils in the school and proportion of pupils entitled to free school meals were small, but there were more new heads who were female (nearly two-thirds of new heads but only one-half of the experienced heads) and an examination of the differences between the distribution of heads by school location revealed that there were fewer inner-city schools and more rural schools with new headteachers.

In our survey of primary schools it was discovered that the outcomes of inspection were not related to the gender of the school's headteacher. Nor were there differences in the 'satisfaction' scores of heads in rural, urban and suburban schools, but heads in inner-city schools had less faith in the usefulness of their inspection than others. As there were fewer new heads in inner-city schools, the analysis was rerun without them to see if the difference could still be detected. In fact, only 1 in 12 of the new heads in the sample but 1 in 6 established heads were in inner-city schools and the difference between new and established heads remained significant when the inner-city headteachers had been removed from both samples. It was concluded that the less positive response of inner-city heads was not sufficient to explain the difference in the response of new and established heads to the survey questions about the verbal feedback, the written report and attitude to inspection.

Heads' reactions to the inspectors' key issues

A further check on this finding was made by looking at heads' reactions to their school's key issues. The heads had been asked to report the number of key issues for action (KIs) which had appeared in the inspectors' final report and to say how many they felt were important. This proportion was calculated for every head in the sample and used as a measure of satisfaction with the outcomes of the report. The proportion of their key issues which new headteachers perceived to be important was larger and the difference between new and established heads was statistically significant. This added further weight to the evidence about new and established heads' differing attitudes to inspection and faith in their inspection findings. New headteachers, we conclude, are more positive about the inspection of their school than more experienced heads and the differences between the two samples are very unlikely to have occurred by chance. Many experienced heads, we suspect, will not be at all surprised by this finding because they will have recognised the extent to which they, themselves, have felt threatened by the prospect of an inspection. It seems, therefore, that those who can distance themselves from responsibility for the outcomes of an inspection can more readily accept its criticisms. New heads like to see themselves as the saviours of run-down, mismanaged schools but a good inspection report can make this a difficult stance to adopt. Nor does it help new heads to stamp their imprint on their schools because staff who feel that they have been successful are less likely to be convinced of the need for change. The point is illustrated in an interview with a headteacher who was soon to leave her present primary school to take up a new post in a school that had been scheduled for inspection a few months after her arrival. She explained why she was hoping for a 'strong' inspection report:

My concern with the next one is that it would be nice to have a good strong OfSTED report. You can use that. I don't want a 'wishy washy' one because, having visited the school, I am aware of areas for development and I don't want those 'washed' over. You have to have this balance to take a school forward. You don't want something too harsh which upsets your staff but you don't want something 'wishy washy' which does not give you enough to pull the school forward.

When pressed to say what she meant by 'a strong report' the head responded, 'It needs to be strong in the sense of negatively strong. It has got to have some meat about it, doesn't it?'

Do heads determine the reactions of teaching staff?

New and established heads were equally likely to report that their school had suffered a lull in activity after the inspection or what has come to be called 'post-inspection blues'. Nearly nine out of ten primary headteachers reported a phase after inspection in which staff found it difficult to rekindle enthusiasm and the school encountered increased absenteeism and exhaustion among teachers. This may last for only a few weeks but one in five primary heads reported a six-month-long lull and one in six reported that the reaction was so severe that it could still be detected a whole year or more after the inspection. The finding is confirmed by research commissioned by OfSTIN (Brunel University CEPPP and Helix Consulting, 1999) which noted that after an inspection 'prolonged tiredness, lack of motivation and low morale' (p.57) affected schools with good and even with 'outstandingly good' inspection reports.

Established heads, in our primary survey, reported average recovery times of five months compared with a mean value of 4½ months for new headteachers, but the difference was not statistically significant. It is concluded, therefore, that the time taken to recover from 'post-inspection blues' does not depend crucially on whether the school has a new or an established head. Information was also gathered about heads' reports of teachers' reactions in the immediate post-inspection period but no information was collected from the teachers themselves. Despite the fact that new and established heads view inspection differently, their reports of the reactions of teaching staff did not differ (see Ferguson *et al.*, 1999b). How heads present the outcomes of inspection to staff and how their own disappointment and satisfaction influence teachers' experience of the inspection are questions that cannot be commented on directly without further research. It does seem, however, that having a new head who views the inspection process positively does not have much influence on the reactions of staff.

Evidence to support this view was sought by looking at another reaction of members of staff in schools with new and established heads. In two-thirds of the entire sample of 363 primary schools, at least one member of the teaching staff had left the school in the twelve-month period since the inspection took place. In over one-third of these schools, headteachers reported that the member of staff who had left had done so as a result of the inspection. A very successful inspection may lead to a good teacher or head being promoted to a post in another school and, on rare occasions, the publicity given to excellent OfSTED inspection reports can lead to the dismantling of successful teaching teams when several staff gain promotion and leave the school. In most cases, however, resignations are the result of failure and disillusionment which, headteachers point out, can affect good teachers but are more likely to affect those who feel that the inspection had become a defeat or an intolerable strain. In fact, new heads were more likely to lose a member of staff but the differences were small and add further support to the hypothesis that the head's reaction to the inspection is *not* a major determinant of staff morale.

Heads talk in confidence to the RgI

The finding that teachers in schools with new and experienced heads were equally likely to leave for reasons associated with the inspection itself was unexpected. It might be assumed that the tendency for new heads to express satisfaction with the findings of their report would help staff to recover more quickly from the effects of the inspection. New heads were also expected to be more likely to have a positive effect on the morale of staff and it was predicted that fewer teachers in schools with new heads would feel so anxious that they decided to leave. Neither of these hypotheses could be sustained possibly because they took too little account of the strength of feeling and powerful emotions which inspections can provoke in teaching staff. They also failed to take account of the extent to which heads appeared to volunteer potentially damaging information to the registered inspector (RgI) and seem, on occasions, to be using the inspection to bring pressure to bear on staff who are felt to be underperforming or who do not fit 'the philosophy of the school'. Our research showed that some heads in secondary schools saw their inspection as a short-cut method of persuading poorly performing staff to leave the school (see Fidler *et al.*, 1998). New heads, perhaps with fewer feelings of loyalty, were a little more inclined to talk to their RgI about poorly performing staff. Several new and established heads expressed disappointment that the OfSTED team had not fully supported their own critical assessment of particular members of staff. However, the data suggest that experienced heads are more circumspect and over one-third of them, but only one-fifth of new heads, said that they had not volunteered any information about their school's weaknesses to the RgI.

New heads and school management

New heads' more positive stance is possibly the result of their ability to approach the inspection more receptively and without the strong sense of involvement and ownership which prevents other heads from sharing their perspective. They are likely to be more open about weaknesses, more approving of the outcomes of inspection and, as a result, more likely to act on their inspection team's recommendations. It might be argued that their greater acceptance of their inspection team's judgement is, on occasions, naïve and that more experienced heads, who have a better understanding of their school, are more realistic. Equally, new heads' greater acceptance of the findings of their inspection report might be explained, in part, by their desire to exorcise the past and establish their leadership in the changed environment which they hope will be more easily created after an inspection. An OfSTED inspection is a good opportunity for new heads to stamp their imprint on the school and, as the head of a secondary school explained, strong ownership of the report depended less on the head's personal feelings about the value of the key issues identified than on the fact that the inspection report had acted as an incentive for staff to review their practice. New heads were often keen to grasp the opportunity that this provided and to use the inspectors' findings as a catalyst for the introduction of the changes that *they* wanted to see being implemented in the school.

Whatever their motivation, it might be expected that new heads would be more open to the inspectors' suggestions and act more promptly on them. Established heads, on the other hand, perceive their responsibilities differently. Hall and Southworth state that: 'The inspection was not only an external audit of the school's strengths and weaknesses, it was also, because of the heads' strong identification with the school, a professional and personal assessment of themselves' (1997, pp.157–8). Experienced heads were not looking for a tool for change and did not feel the same need for an external audit. They were in a stronger position to reject some of the recommendations of their inspection report that were not in line with the school's values because they could usually depend on the support of the school community.

It has already been noted that some new heads like to think of their predecessors as less competent managers with the occasional hint that the gulf between them reflects the differences between modern and outmoded management styles. As one new head remarked: 'I was aware of many weak areas, having taken over from a headteacher who had been in post for 22 years and had a particular style of management and vision of the school.'

New heads may embrace inspection as an opportunity to make an impact on the school's problems and prepare the ground for the management of changes which might otherwise have proved difficult to introduce. This provides a meeting point for the aspirations of new heads and inspection teams but it is an approach which cannot easily be converted to the school's advantage without the support of staff. Some new heads discovered that OfSTED inspection impairs their ability to persuade others to follow their lead. One head, describing a six-month-long lull in activity in her school, noted: 'As a new headteacher I was enthusiastic and wanted to get on with my new role, but staff needed a rest.' Another new head, unable to motivate the staff after the inspection, reported: 'I deliberately took my foot off the throttle for a couple of terms.' A new head in a school that had been given a very good inspection report commented: 'Even with such a good report, I was surprised how low the staff were for at least two terms.'

Dunning (1996) investigated new primary heads' management problems and ranked them according to the number who perceived them as serious difficulties. 'Dealing with poor teacher morale', 'supporting ineffective teachers', 'getting teachers to accept new ideas' and 'dealing with teachers' negative reactions' were ranked in the top 20. All of them are important challenges for new heads which are almost certain to have a major influence on the quality and pace of new development, but they are also difficulties which are likely to be exacerbated by inspection. It seems that OfSTED inspection, while aiming to assist schools in their development, has the unintended effect of temporarily demotivating staff and thus impairing their headteachers' ability to lead, at least in the short term.

The reactions of new and established heads to inspection raise questions about whose interests the inspectors are serving. New heads may well feel that their interests have been served if the report contains a sufficient number of critical comments, but this is not likely to be a point of view that is shared by their teacher colleagues. In Chapter 12 we examine the implications of the emphasis that OfSTED places on public accountability and the role that inspection teams play in helping schools to improve. These two functions or purposes of inspection, we will argue, are often incompatible. New headteachers may believe that an inspection can serve their self-interest and encourage them in their efforts to bring about improvements in their new school. Established heads, however, are probably right to recognise that inspection is a 'high stakes' game in which there are few consolations for those who lose. Parents should be aware that the process can cause disruption to their children's education both before and after the inspection and that their children's teachers (including those who receive positive feedback from the inspectors) are likely to experience adverse reactions to the stress and exhaustion which often accompany an inspection. The implications of the tension between OfSTED's accountability and school improvement functions are discussed in greater detail in the final chapters of this book where we argue that inspection should change so that it can be perceived by all heads and school staff as an approach which has school improvement much higher on its agenda.

Professional issues for discussion

- How can heads – new or experienced – best capitalise on the opportunities for change brought about by inspection?
- 'Post-inspection blues' appears to be a common phenomenon, but how can its worst effects be minimised?
- If inspection is such a 'high stakes' game, how much information about the school's strengths and weaknesses should be revealed to the inspectors?

7

OfSTED and the governing body

Before discussing the findings of our research as far as the inspection process and governing bodies are concerned, it is worth asking the basic question – 'for whom is the inspection carried out and the resulting inspection report produced?' In evidence to the House of Commons Select Committee into OfSTED inspections – whose main findings are mentioned in the next chapter – Pat Petch, Chair of the National Governors Council, remarked that she had never been entirely clear who the audience for inspection was, asking, 'Is it actually a report for parents? Is it actually a report for the governing body? Is it a report for the headteacher?' (House of Commons, 1999a, p.36). Of course, it can be for all three, but it is very difficult to produce a single report that is tailored to meet the needs of all parties. Certainly, as the Select Committee notes, there is evidence that governors are more in favour of and have more confidence in OfSTED inspections than the heads and the teachers in the schools that they govern. However, it is not entirely clear whether an OfSTED inspection is an inspection of the school *and* its governing body, or whether it is undertaken largely *for* the governing body – the post-OfSTED action plan is after all referred to as the governors' action plan.

Governing body reaction and response to inspection, however, has not been uniform. The Institution for School and College Governors (ISCG, 1996) notes that governing bodies have reacted very differently to inspection – both to its purpose and to the process: 'In many schools it has been used as an improvement *tool* or yardstick, whereas in others it has been viewed more like a *weapon* inflicting both pain and damage' (ISCG, 1996, p.1). In many cases it has had the unintended consequence of uniting governors and the school against a perceived, common, outside force.

This chapter begins by examining what inspectors look for as far as the governing body is concerned and notes the evidence on which their judgements are based. Information from the surveys and the case studies is used to examine the governing body's role in the formulation of the post-OfSTED action plan and monitoring of the key issues. The extent to which governor involvement in their schools has changed and the role that inspection has played is considered before finally returning to the issue of monitoring. It is suggested that in many cases inspection has been beneficial because it has forced the governing body to be more involved in the life of the school. It has also helped to focus governors' efforts and energies on improving the standards and quality of education provided by their schools. The chapter concludes by noting that monitoring (the most problematic of governors' many roles) is distinct from inspection. There is a danger, however, of the two activities being seen as similar and of governors adopting an inspectorial role – a role which it is argued is seen by many, including governors, as inappropriate (Creese and Earley, 1999; House of Commons, 1999b).

What do inspectors look for?

As far as the functioning of the governing body is concerned, what do inspectors look for during the course of an inspection? This is not as easy to answer as it may at first appear. Certainly, the Framework for the inspection of schools states that the Registered Inspector's report should include 'an evaluation of the strategic management of the resources available to the school, including an assessment of the work of the governing body and appropriate staff' (OfSTED,1994/5). In addition, the school is judged by the inspectors in terms of the leadership shown by the governing body and the effectiveness of the working relationship between governors and the school. The OfSTED handbook notes that the inspectors' report should also include 'an evaluation of the effectiveness of the governing body in fulfilling its legal responsibilities' (OfSTED, 1994/5).

A detailed analysis of specific references to governors in OfSTED inspection reports has been undertaken by Creese (1997) who found much variation in practice. Evidence on which inspectors based their judgements was likely to be derived from a variety of sources, including interviews with governors – often involving the lay inspector, the chair and/or the chairs of committees. Evidence was hardly ever derived from the observation of governing body meetings. Creese's main finding was that 'there is still considerable variation in the length and detail of the section of the report devoted to the work of the governing body' (1997, p.17) although there is 'a sufficient number of common themes and phrases which run through the reports to suggest that a clearer view of what is expected of an effective governing body is now emerging from OfSTED' (1997, p.17).

More recently, with reference to various sources, including his own surveys, OfSTED official publications and the chief inspector's annual reports, Creese (1999) has produced a picture of what OfSTED perceives to be an effective governing body. He concludes that the role of the governing body as expounded in *Governing Bodies and Effective Schools* (DfE/OfSTED, 1995a) is the dominant or preferred model. In this publication, the governing body's role is couched in terms of three key areas: providing a strategic view, acting as a critical friend and ensuring accountability. Indeed, it was the first area – that of acting strategically – which inspectors were specifically requested to comment on in their inspection reports for the spring term of 1998. For that term (and that term only) governing bodies were graded by the inspectors on a seven-point scale in relation to the degree to which they were fulfilling their strategic role. Inspectors were given no formal guidance from OfSTED on exactly how they should make their judgements, although broad criteria were offered for the achievement of grades 2, 4 and 6 (OfSTED, 1997a). An analysis by OfSTED of the inspectors' grades of the 2,360 schools inspected in the spring term of 1998 showed that three-quarters of their governing bodies were 'satisfactory' or better, with secondary school governing bodies emerging as slightly better in the area of self-review (of their operation) than were those of primary schools (Creese and Earley, 1999). There is work currently taking place within OfSTED which may well lead to a clearer delineation of what inspectors perceive as the main purpose of governors and the characteristics of an effective governing body. As OfSTED note: 'The new inspection requirements will focus even more sharply on the work of the governing body given their increasing responsibilities' (House of Commons, 1999c, p.27).

What is clear is that OfSTED inspections are one of the ways in which it is being made increasingly apparent to governing bodies that they have an important role to play in raising standards and a responsibility to ensure that their school is operating successfully. The recently acquired statutory requirement to set targets for pupil attainment has added to this sense of responsibility (DfEE, 1997b; Creese and Earley, 1999). Similarly, evidence from schools which have 'failed' their inspection and become subject to special measures shows that in many cases governing bodies have become more effective, making better use of the limited time available and assisting their school to come off the special measures register (DfEE, 1997c; Earley, 1997; OfSTED, 1997b, 1999a). The very existence of OfSTED and the process of external inspection has, according to one governor training organisation, 'empowered governing bodies, enabling them to gain entry into legitimate areas of concern which had otherwise been closed to them' (House of Commons, 1999a, p.35). A credible and accurate audit of the school and its governing body can provide invaluable information for those wishing to bring about change. Inspection is said to be encouraging more governing bodies to give serious consideration to how they and their schools are performing; it has the potential to empower them and can act as a powerful stimulus or catalyst for change (Creese, 1997; Gann, 1997; Earley, 1998a). Were such trends equally apparent in the governing bodies of the schools involved in research? What were the levels of governor involvement in the inspection process, particularly after the inspection and the post-OfSTED action planning phase?

The governing body's post–OfSTED action plan

The immediate task of the governing body after the inspection is to attend the feedback session given by the Registered Inspector and then to work with the headteacher on the post-OfSTED action plan. After the immediate euphoria, relief and celebration of 'having survived OfSTED', a period of 'post-inspection blues' or depression frequently followed (see Chapter 6). The ISCG see this possible under-performance as needing to be dealt with through careful strategic planning in which governors have an important role. The governing body not only needs to be aware of a possible dip in performance (which as our research suggests may last for six months or more) but must also be 'ready to suggest strategies to deal with staff morale and absence, pupil unrest, lack of energy for initiatives and so forth' (ISCG, 1996, p.4).

Governing bodies, regardless of the outcome of the inspection, need to provide support for staff who invariably find the inspection process stressful. Heads and senior staff will, most likely, have the immediate task of re-motivating staff and will look to the governing body to approve the resources and provide the necessary support to enable the school to progress. This may take the form of agreeing spending on training or simply being available to talk with staff, particularly senior staff, as and when needed (Creese and Earley, 1999).

The governing body is legally responsible for ensuring the preparation and implementation of the post-OfSTED action plan which has to be produced within 40 days of receipt of the inspector's report. The fact that governing bodies rather than heads or LEAs take responsibility for the post-OfSTED action plan is entirely consistent with their position as the body legally responsible for the strategic and resource management of the school. The legislation states that the governing body must draw up the action plan after the inspection. Although we found examples where this was a combined or joint effort (see also Creese and Earley, 1999), it was nearly always taken to mean that the task was delegated to the head and senior staff. The governors rarely produced the action plan themselves (an example of where this did happen is given later) although they must ensure that it is completed within the required timescale. These plans turn the key issues for action (see Chapter 5) into proposals which are timetabled, resourced and usually have named persons responsible for their implementation.

The post-OfSTED action plans of the case study schools in our research were found to have a similar format. For example, a typical primary school action plan devoted each of its numbered sections to a separate key issue. Plans often consisted of six broad columns spread across one side of A4 paper (i.e. 'landscape' rather than 'portrait'). The titles at the top of each column might be: (i) Action to be taken, (ii) People responsible for action, (iii) Arrangements for monitoring, (iv) Target date for completion, (v) Performance indicators and success criteria and, finally, (vi) Resources for implementation. Some plans had a separate column or section for details of any in-service education or training (INSET) required for staff. Although the length of the plan depended to some extent on the number of key issues listed in the report, plans were rarely more than ten pages long and typically consisted of a front sheet giving the school's name and address and the date of the inspection and, without further description or preamble, five pages (usually one for each key issue) describing the action to be taken.

Our study shows that the level of governing body involvement in their schools varied considerably but for some it had changed since the school's inspection. This can be seen in relation to governors' contribution to their school's post-OfSTED action plan and to their general levels of involvement in the school. Our surveys of both primary and secondary schools asked heads, using a six–point scale, to assess the contribution that governors had made to the post-OfSTED action plan. Tables 7.1 and 7.2, summarise the

Table 7.1 Secondary heads' perceptions of governors' contributions to the post-OfSTED action plans

	1 no contribution	2	3	4	5	6 major contribution
Survey 1993	9%	36%	20%	21%	8%	6%
Survey 1994	11%	28%	20%	21%	14%	5%
Survey 1996	7%	21%	19%	28%	16%	9%

1993: N = 170 (60% response)
1994: N = 252 (63% response)
1996: N = 305 (80% response)

Table 7.2 Primary heads' perceptions of governors' contributions to the post-OfSTED action plans

	1 no contribution	2	3	4	5	6 major contribution
Survey A (spring 1998)	20%	26%	18%	16%	14%	7%
Survey B2 (autumn 1998)	9%	33%	19%	20%	14%	5%

Survey A: N = 369 (75% response)
Survey B2: N = 309 (88% response)

findings of the three secondary surveys (1993, 1994 and 1996) and the two primary surveys (spring and autumn 1998).

The data show that, over the years, governors have (at least according to heads) *increased* their contribution to the action planning process and the percentage of governing bodies making little or no contribution has been falling. In the first survey of secondary schools (inspected in 1993), 45 per cent were reported to be making little or no contribution to the post-OfSTED action plan compared to 39 per cent in 1994 and only 28 per cent in 1996. Table 7.1 also shows that in 1996 one-quarter of respondents reported that governors had made a major contribution compared with only 14 per cent in 1993.

Table 7.2 shows that of the primary heads in Survey A, nearly one-half (46 per cent) rated the governing body's contribution to the action plan in the lowest two categories of this six-point scale. One in five chose the lowest category of all, indicating that the governors made 'no contribution' to the post-OfSTED action plan. In the later of our two primary surveys, just over four out of ten heads (42 per cent) also rated governors' contributions in the lowest two categories but only one in ten (9 per cent) noted that the governors made no contribution whatsoever. The table also shows that about one-fifth of primary school heads reported that governors had made a major contribution to the action plan.

It seems increasingly that governors are less likely to believe that everything can be left to the head but, judging by both primary and secondary heads' perceptions of the governing body's contribution to the post-OfSTED action plan, there is a very wide range of practice among governing bodies. (Examples from the case study schools are given in the next two sections.) Most heads assess the governors' contribution as a relatively minor one but with a trend to greater involvement over time. This has been attributed to the influence of inspection on governors' assumptions about the extent of their responsibilities (Earley, 1998a). It is interesting to note the differences between the phases with secondary school governors showing an overall greater contribution to action planning than their primary counterparts; a trend supported by other recent research which suggests secondary school governing bodies generally saw themselves as more effective than did those from primary schools (Scanlon, Earley and Evans, 1999).

Heads were also asked about the extent to which the inspection had altered governor involvement in the school (see Table 7.3). Again, this was said to have changed. In 1996 (the only year in which this question was asked of the secondary schools) four out of ten secondary heads reported that they considered the inspection had *increased* the involvement of governors. The corresponding figure was even higher for the primary surveys (43 per cent and 48 per cent respectively). It is also worth noting the large number of heads who recorded 'no change' with many explaining that their governors were already heavily involved in their schools.

Table 7.3   The extent to which governor involvement in the school has changed

	1 decreased	2	3 no change	4	5 increased
Secondary survey	1%	0%	59%	31%	9%
Primary survey A	2%	3%	51%	31%	13%
Primary survey B2	1%	3%	48%	32%	16%

Secondary survey (1996) N = 305
Primary survey A (spring 1998) N = 374; Survey B2 (autumn 1998) N = 311

Governor involvement in schools

The effects of inspection and governor involvement in the post-inspection action plan and in school life generally were further explored in the research. Examples from the projects are given separately for each school phase.

Secondary schools

Some secondary heads noted how they had been able to use the inspection report to bring about change in the way the governing body operated. In some cases the findings had helped to put pressure on the governors to increase their visits to the school or become more involved in monitoring policies. A direct result of inspection was that governors were said to be becoming even more aware of their responsibilities and the work of the school and its performance.

Others noted how, as far as governor involvement was concerned, inspection had either speeded things up or slowed them down. These comments included:

> The change was happening anyway but a criticism stung a few into greater involvement.

> The report actually suggested that governors should be more involved but no action has been taken, they are if anything less involved.

> OfSTED's criticism of my governors made my two best ones leave – a disaster!

Not all secondary heads welcomed the increased governor involvement which inspection was said to have encouraged. One head noted how his governors were now 'involved in almost everything' while another felt that the governing body was already over-involved in the day-to-day management of the school.

Many interviewees described how governors had been involved in helping to draw up post-OfSTED action plans, usually by setting up small working groups with staff who would draft the initial response. For example, in one secondary school a small strategic group had been established which approved the draft action plan before it went to the General Management Committee (made up of the chairs of various committees) and then, finally, to the full governing body. Governors were also involved in various capacities in monitoring progress made on the key issues for action. Others noted how their governing body was more involved in monitoring and although this was usually on the finance front, more governors were becoming involved in monitoring the curriculum.

Another head claimed the school's governors were still operating in 'pre-1986 mode' (the 1986 Education Act changed the roles and increased the responsibilities of governing bodies) and that this weakness had been identified by the inspectors. However, the inspection was said not to have made much difference (for example, not all the governors had attended the feedback). The governors were said to be 'good folk who mean well but were not competent to do the job'. Their passive role meant that they did not know what was going on in the school, but as the head remarked, 'it could be worse, I suppose, as they could be interfering!'

A very different picture of governor involvement was given by a head in a neighbouring authority. Governors had been involved in addressing the key issues in the action plan and through the committee structure had already participated in the school development plan (SDP) and knew of the school's targets. This governing body had arranged two extra meetings in the week so the inspectors could attend. The action plan targets were apportioned to teams of governors so that they could look at what was being done and how it was to be achieved. In this school one of the action plan targets had been taken over completely by the governors who had been into the school to interview staff and work up ideas and suggestions. The key issue centred on the involvement of middle managers – post-holders were to be given more opportunities to be involved in whole-school decision-making. The head remarked that he had disagreed with the registered inspector over this issue so it was thought to be a good idea to give this key issue to the governing body: to enable them to go and talk to whoever they liked and to report back on what needed to be done to provide more opportunities for middle managers to be involved in decision-making. Governors were also linked to other targets to make sure they were being implemented. As the head noted: 'It's a level of involvement that you don't often see in governing bodies.'

Levels of involvement of governing bodies did differ significantly; in some cases heads were content with this, in others they would have welcomed a greater degree of involvement. A head of a grammar school, for example, remarked that her governors had contributed little to the action plan but that did not mean to say they were not involved.

> My governors are very involved in everything but they say to me 'Right Mary you put it all together and we'll have a look at it.' So I dutifully do that and they pull it all to pieces and put their own stamp on it. We work well together

and I enjoy talking to them – everything is talked through but it's my blueprint if you like in every respect. The governing body is effective – this was noted in the report – and we get on well but they leave me to get on to a large extent, perhaps more so than I would like. I don't want them to interfere but to get into classrooms more. We are appreciative of what is done and they have tremendous expertise but they are very busy people. Their own jobs keep them away from school during the day. So I would like them to have better first-hand knowledge of what's going on in school.

Primary schools

Primary school governors explained that they were involved in discussions of the implications of the inspection report but usually expected the head and senior staff to produce a draft action plan for their approval. The draft plan was discussed at governors' meetings (both in committees and full governing body meetings) when suggestions were made and incorporated as amendments to the final version of the post-OfSTED action plan. The responsibility for its implementation was also delegated by the governing body to those who were seen to be in the best position to implement its provisions, namely the head and the school's teaching and administrative staff. Governors did, however, receive regular progress reports on the implementation of the plan and reported that they contributed actively to monitoring progress on the key issues. Where a governor had been given responsibility for specific parts of the curriculum or for monitoring a particular key issue, this sometimes meant observing teachers in their classrooms.

In one of the case studies, the governors decided to apply a literal interpretation to the requirements of the Education (Schools) Act 1992 (see Circular 7/93, p.8 (37)) and wrote the post-OfSTED action plan themselves. This caused a serious conflict with the school's headteacher (see later). Few governing bodies exerted their legal rights to the complete ownership of the action planning process but, as within the secondary sector, levels of involvement did vary.

In most cases governors played a role in post-inspection action planning which could best be described as supervision of the process, but some governing bodies were merely helpful bystanders or interested spectators. For example, the chair of governors in a small rural school felt that when a school had 'a very good head' the governors should be 'helpful when needed' but should 'show trust' and 'leave her to do her job'. The head of that school believed that the governors realised that they did not do enough and added:

> Because the report that we received was good, the governors that were involved patted themselves on the back and said, 'Well we knew you would be all right. As regards action plans and everything, it is better if you get on with it' (head of a rural school).

Some governors who were made aware of the full range of their responsibilities during the inspection were not happy about being criticised by

OfSTED inspectors. One governing body had been stung into action by a critical comment from the RgI and was still upset about it a year or more after the inspection. It had made the chair of the governing body aware of the difficulty of asking people to volunteer help and then criticising them for not fulfilling their responsibilities satisfactorily.

> The report to the governors was quite abrupt and many governors were hurt and quite upset. You would need to go a long way before you found governors who do more for their school. They are volunteers at the end of the day and they give a lot of time (chair of governors of a rural school).

The chair of the curriculum committee at the same school had not attended the feedback session with the RgI but had been interviewed during inspection week and noted what he believed was another contradiction in the inspectors' position.

> Her (the RgI's) response was, 'You must realise that you have a statutory responsibility for the delivery of the curriculum in the classroom. It's what you should be doing.' It was almost as if she was quoting. If her perception was that the chair of the Curriculum Committee was not on top of how the curriculum was delivered in the classroom, then she was quite right. But it's always going to be the case isn't it? (chair of curriculum committee).

A chair of governors of an inner-city school made similar points but was, by contrast, very pleased with the way the inspectors had handled their meetings with governors.

> They were very open and very professional. They understood that we are lay people giving our time voluntarily. They knew that we could not answer specific questions on, say, curriculum matters but they knew how to get the answers out of us. If the RgI had said, 'How do you monitor the curriculum?' I would have said, 'Oh my God, how do I monitor the curriculum?' It's how they phrased the questions. . . . Do you sit in classrooms? . . . Do you have responsibility for particular areas of the curriculum? (chair of governors).

A particularly interesting example was found in one of the case studies where relationships between the head and the governing body had become strained. The school had been categorised as one with 'serious weaknesses' and the head and governing body were in conflict during the post-OfSTED action planning process. The head remarked:

> The governors are trying to play my role. I wanted to take it (the action plan) and finish it but one or two very active governors took it off to the pub with their laptops. It was taken out of my hands (head of an urban school).

The head discovered that protests to LEA officers did not have any effect. The LEA reportedly described the problem as being 'in a grey area' and, unsurprisingly, given the governors' legal rights in such matters, senior LEA colleagues were unwilling to intervene or ask the governing body to adopt a more conventional approach to action planning. This example of conflict was in sharp contrast to the usually positive relationship between heads and governors described by the governors in the other case study schools.

The headteacher presents us with documents for approval. There may be some discussion but as in government everything that the prime minister wants to get through does get through (governor of a rural primary school).

The governing body left the action plan to the senior managers but the action plan was presented to parents by the governing body. I saw it in draft form before it was fleshed out by the senior management team (governor of an inner-city primary school).

Governors and monitoring

Comments from heads and governors from both primary and secondary schools point to the role that governors are increasingly playing in relation to monitoring (particularly but not exclusively of the post-OfSTED action plan) and in visiting classrooms and observing lessons. In some schools, governors may also be involved as part of review and evaluation teams investigating various aspects of the curriculum (for examples of this practice, see Creese and Earley, 1999). If schools are becoming 'self-inspecting' and more concerned with monitoring and evaluating their own performance, does this mean governors will increasingly see themselves, and be seen by others, as having an inspectorial role? Is the governing body expected to act, like the head, as the 'inspector within' or the 'inspector in residence' (OfSTED, 1999a, p.40), monitoring school and teacher performance and ensuring the implementation of government policy?

The governing body's role in monitoring and evaluating is one of the most difficult and least understood aspects of its work. Generally, however, research suggests governors feel content with the part they play in monitoring and evaluating the school's finances and its physical environment but less so with other matters. Traditionally, as Joan Sallis and others have noted, governors have felt more comfortable 'looking into lavatories' rather than 'looking into learning' (Creese and Earley, 1999; Earley, 2000). The curriculum – the school's core business – and its monitoring is still seen as predominantly a matter for the professionals and not for the lay governing body. Governors often express doubts, not only about whether they possess the skills and knowledge to monitor and evaluate, but, indeed, whether it is their place to do it at all.

Monitoring is the act of checking progress to ensure plans and intentions are underway. It is not the same as inspection although the term, and to a lesser extent, evaluation, is often associated with it. Evaluation involves a process of data collection and analysis to form judgements about the value or worth of an activity. Governing bodies are seen as responsible for monitoring post-OfSTED action plans, school improvement and development plans, financial performance, policy implementation and the standards of achievement of the pupils (Creese and Earley, 1999). To be able to do this effectively, the governing body must know and understand what the school is trying to achieve. They also need information about the school and the ability to interpret that information. Governing bodies usually undertake their monitoring and evaluating responsibilities through a combination of 'walking and talking', links with curricular and pastoral systems, reports to the governing body from the head and other professionals, and governor visits to the school in session (Earley, 2000).

In a study of effective governance, Creese and Earley (1999) note the generally held view that it was unhelpful for governors to take over responsibility for day-to-day monitoring. Governors appreciated that 'professional monitoring' is the job of the school's managers but governors need to be kept informed of what systems of monitoring and evaluation are being used and whether they are effective. They add:

> There is a danger of governors having too great an involvement in day-to-day monitoring or trying to adopt an inspectorial role. Governors and teachers need to be clear about the purposes of the exercise, how evidence is to be gathered and how that evidence will be used. . . . It must also be remembered that the majority of governors are lay people with limited experience of educational practice and hence may not be in a position to be able to make informed (professional) judgments on teaching methods. Governors are after all lay people and their strength has always been seen in these terms (Creese and Earley, 1999, p.71).

The degree to which governors are involved in the process of evidence collection will vary from one governing body to another, but it will also depend on the area to be monitored and evaluated. For some matters, governors may be directly involved (e.g. evaluating the school's health and safety policy, a curriculum review or audit) but in most instances it is more likely to be a case of the governing body asking questions of the professionals (e.g. for progress reports in relation to the SDP or the post-OfSTED action plan). Governing bodies have a responsibility to ensure that both monitoring and evaluation are being carried out by the professionals – an area of school activity which OfSTED reports frequently identify as key issues for action and in need of improvement (see Chapter 5). If the professionals are seen as being generally weak in this area (OfSTED, 1998b), it is perhaps unsurprising that some governors have difficulty in understanding and enacting this aspect of their role.

Is there a danger, in fulfilling their monitoring role in the ways being suggested by OfSTED and others, of governors becoming seen, rightly or wrongly, as mini-inspectors? Is their role increasingly seen as one of surveillance, of checking up on the school's activities, particularly its teachers? Interestingly, where schools have introduced structured programmes of classroom visits by governors, teacher reaction has tended to be positive (Creese and Earley, 1999; Scanlon, Earley and Evans, 1999). The Select Committee's report on *The Role of the Governing Body* (House of Commons, 1999b) highlighted the importance of governors visiting schools, but as a representative of one of the headteacher associations remarked, the purpose of such visits must be 'part of the corporate business of school governors' and not an opportunity to adopt an 'OfSTED-type role with a clipboard' when visiting classrooms (ibid., p.27).

Any moves to encourage a greater degree of school self-evaluation – generally considered to be an effective route to school improvement (see Chapter 11) – should, in some way, involve governors (and other stakeholders). MacBeath, for example, has discussed governors' roles in school self-evaluation and this includes monitoring (MacBeath, Boyd and Rand, 1996).

Certainly governors themselves are very conscious of 'not wanting to trespass on the job of the professionals', often emphasising that 'after all, that's what they're paid for!'

Concluding comment

The 1998 Standards and Framework Act sees the purpose of governing bodies as helping to provide the best possible education for the pupils in their schools. This is to be achieved in a number of ways but in any delineation of the roles and responsibilities of governing bodies that of monitoring and evaluation is usually given prominence. Governing bodies are being asked to play an even greater role in monitoring and evaluating school performance and in raising standards of achievement, particularly by promoting a climate of improvement. As we have noted, inspection has led to a growing number of governors becoming more involved in their schools and more aware of their responsibilities. Indeed, there is a growing body of evidence, from our own studies and elsewhere, to support the view that inspection has the potential to empower the governing body by making it more aware of the nature and extent of its responsibilities, and in particular to sharpen the monitoring role (Earley, 1998a).

The governing body is now expected to work collaboratively on such matters as policy formation, action planning, monitoring, evaluation and review, and to play an increasing role in target-setting and school improvement. Very few governing bodies would now claim to play only a symbolic role in the life of the school (Scanlon, Earley and Evans, 1999). Indeed, Creese (1999) discusses the possible growth of an orthodoxy, generated by OfSTED, of what an effective governing body consists of, which he suggests, along with inspection itself, might be 'an attempt to ensure all governing bodies operate in the same manner and with similar agendas' (p.250).

Monitoring and inspecting *are* different activities, but for many governors and teachers the distinction is not always as clear as it should be. There still exists some confusion about the governing body's role in monitoring and evaluating and a lack of clarity regarding the exact nature and importance of lay and professional perspectives. As moves develop for schools to become self-evaluating and 'self-inspecting', can we expect there to be similar

pressures on governors to become more inspectorial in the way they operate? Interestingly, both the DfEE and OfSTED were not convinced of the
merits of the Select Committee's suggestion that a governor should become
part of the inspection team, albeit only as an observer (House of Commons,
1999c). Governors have an important monitoring role – an important part of
the process for school 'self-inspection' (see Chapter 12) – but should they
also be seen as unpaid inspectors enforcing government policy? Perhaps we
should leave the last word to the Select Committee which is very clear where
it stands on the matter of governors and inspection:

> We agree with the Government that governors do not have a role in 'inspec-
> ting' work in the classroom. It is the responsibility of the governing body to
> monitor standards of achievement, to be accountable for them and to ensure
> that weaknesses are addressed. However, it is not helpful for individual gover-
> nors to use this responsibility as the basis for inspecting individual teachers
> (House of Commons, 1999b, p.27).

Professional issues for discussion

- To what degree and in which areas should governors be expected to become
  actively and directly involved in the monitoring process?
- Is a governor's direct role in monitoring aspects of the school's performance
  comparable to the role of the lay inspector in an OfSTED inspection?
- Is it time for the lay perspective of the governing body, always seen as its
  fundamental strength, to be re-emphasised to avoid any possible misunder-
  standings or confusion?
- Is there a danger of OfSTED producing an orthodoxy of an effective governing
  body which 'ensures all governing bodies operate in the same manner and with
  similar agendas' (Creese, 1999, p.250)?

8

Improving inspection: the views of heads, inspectors and the Select Committee

Our survey of registered inspectors (RgIs) and the follow-up survey of primary heads asked both groups to comment on some of the strengths and weaknesses of the inspection system (as it then was in 1998). The surveys also sought advice about improvements that heads and RgIs would like to be introduced in the future. Each questionnaire took advantage of the fact that, at the time of the surveys, the House of Commons Select Committee on the work of OfSTED had just begun to take evidence (November 1998). The samples of primary heads and RgIs were asked exactly the same question:

> The House of Commons Select Committee is currently meeting to consider the future of OfSTED inspections. It will be asking how inspections might develop in future and how their potential to bring about improvements in schools might be enhanced. Please suggest *two* pieces of advice which you would like to offer the Select Committee.

It was possible, therefore, to identify concerns which were frequently given a high priority by inspectors or heads or both and to distinguish them from those which few of either group believed were very important.

When headteachers were asked to suggest two pieces of advice that they would like to offer to the Select Committee, a wide range of responses was made. The six most frequently mentioned pieces of advice are shown in Table 8.1.

When the same questions were asked of RgIs, there were marked similarities in the responses that were made. As with the sample of heads, the responses were categorised and counted and the six most frequently mentioned pieces of advice given by registered inspectors are listed in Table 8.2.

In January 1999 (about five months before the date of the House of Commons Select Committee published its report on the work of OfSTED), we published our predictions about what that report might conclude (*Times Educational Supplement*, 22 January, 1999). The Select Committee report was published in June 1999 and we have been able to check our predictions and

Table 8.1 Heads' advice to the Select Committee

• Inspectors should follow up inspections and provide support/advice for school improvement	25% (79)
• Less notice of an impending inspection should be given	20% (61)
• LEAs should be involved in inspecting and advising	13% (41)
• Inspectors should have appropriate experience and qualifications	13% (39)
• The focus of inspections should be narrowed	11% (34)
• The experience of being inspected should be made less stressful	10% (32)

Notes: 311 heads provided a total of 614 pieces of advice. Percentages do not add up to 100. In interpreting this information, it should be remembered that the question was open ended and the percentages quoted are not, therefore, the proportions of heads who shared the same points of view but the proportions (with an infinite array of possibilities to choose from) who gave priority to these points.

Table 8.2 Registered inspectors' advice to the Select Committee

• Inspectors should follow up inspections and provide support/advice for school improvement	26% (42)
• Schools' self-evaluation data should be taken into account	22% (35)
• Marketisation of inspection, bids, fees and contractors should be ended	20% (32)
• LEAs should be involved in inspecting and advising	16% (26)
• The focus of inspections should be narrowed	15% (24)
• Inspectors should have appropriate experience and qualifications	14% (22)

Notes: 162 RgIs gave 319 pieces of advice. Percentages do not add up to 100. In interpreting this information, it should be remembered that the question was open ended and the percentages quoted are not, therefore, the proportions of RgIs who shared the same points of view but the proportions (with an infinite array of possibilities to choose from) who gave priority to these points.

discuss the heads' and RgIs' recommendations for improvement in the light of the Select Committee's findings.

Should inspectors advise schools?

Headteachers want the inspection process to make provision for inspection teams to provide help and advice for schools. They recommended that follow-up visits by the RgI should become a recognised feature of the inspection system and agreed that inspectors should not 'hit and run' but should show a continuing interest in the school's progress.

The 1997 survey of secondary schools also provided a list of suggestions for improving inspection and heads indicated, on a six-point scale, the extent to which they believed the change would be a major improvement. When heads responded to the suggestion that inspectors should give advice, one-half of the sample of over 300 secondary heads chose the first category expressing the belief that an advisory role for inspectors would most defi-nitely constitute a major improvement. More than eight in every ten heads chose the first two categories expressing approval for the suggestion. Fewer than one in 20 felt that an advisory role for inspectors would *not* represent an improvement.

The RgIs were also keen to have an opportunity to follow up inspections and give advice to schools. It was their most frequently chosen piece of advice for the Select Committee. They saw their role as making use of the experience gained in inspection to disseminate good practice and 'celebrate success'. They emphasised their value in helping the school to make the most of the inspection and wanted to see opportunities for inspection teams to return to the school after the inspection to offer professional support/ advice and to monitor the progress of action on their advice. One inspector suggested 'the introduction of an additional contract, should the school require it, to allow the inspection team the opportunity to advise on the action plan, etc.'

OfSTED's response to such suggestions would be that there is no reason why a school should not ask inspectors to act as consultants, indeed some have (see Close, 1998), but the point was qualified with the important proviso that, to safeguard schools, inspectors are strongly discouraged from 'touting for trade'. What heads and registered inspectors argue is that the provision of advice for schools should become an established aspect of the inspection process. They believe that the 'link between advice and inspection should be strengthened' or, as one RgI suggested, 'inspectors should avoid situations when teams make judgements, and leave the school unsupported.' Heads frequently made the same point and felt that inspectors ought to wear 'an adviser's hat'. They shared the RgIs' belief that their experience of inspections could be used to help schools to im-prove. Some registered inspectors had fulfilled this function and their efforts had been appreciated. One headteacher described the lead inspec-tor as a 'font of knowledge' and another suggested that OfSTED should 'allow inspection teams to give advice to schools on ways forward. My RgI was brilliant. She gave suggestions I found really useful.' Similarly, the more structured way in which key points for action are now written by some RgIs gives each school more of a steer about how they might be successfully implemented.

Others made the point in a more challenging way and urged the Select Committee to ensure that inspectors were made to be 'more constructive' and 'work with schools and be less confrontational'. Evans and Penney (1994), in a case study of an LEA (entitled 'Whatever happened to good advice'), concluded that the relationship between inspection and advice was 'crucial' and like Wragg (1997) saw the LEA as a vital partner in the process.

> The evidence suggests that there are few merits to the separation of inspection and advice from in-service support, and none whatsoever to the extraction of the latter from LEA control (Evans and Penney, 1994).

We predicted that the House of Commons Select Committee would not want inspectors to become involved in giving schools advice about action planning or school improvement. The routine provision of such support, we argued, would change the nature of the relationship between teachers and inspectors and would subtly but inexorably alter the nature and purpose of inspection. The members, we reasoned, would be well aware that successive governments have perceived inspection's accountability function to be of great political importance and would be unwilling to allow the pressure on poorly performing schools and teachers to be reduced. The Committee actually concluded:

> We do not think that OfSTED inspection teams should become involved in the provision of formal advice or school development. It is not the role of the inspector to come into the school and tell the headteacher how to run it. It is up to the school itself to build on the outcomes of inspection, rather than depending on the inspectors for guidance (House of Commons, 1999a, paragraph 99).

This stance does not seem to be an entirely satisfactory response. If useful advice is available (and heads and RgIs are agreed that it is) and if inspectors want to help (RgIs appear to want a role in supporting school development) then discussions between schools and inspection teams seem to be a mechanism for encouraging improvement. In fact, the Select Committee continues its recommendation:

> OFSTED inspectors can best act as catalysts for change and improvement. This we believe, can best be achieved through the development of a 'professional dialogue' in which the potential benefits of inspection are realised (1999a, paragraph 98).

The two arguably contradictory halves of the recommendation are intended to free inspectors from an advisory role while giving advice if they feel that this is appropriate. The recommendation seems to provide something for everyone but, significantly, begins with a strong statement about the undesirability of inspectors supporting school development. The 'dichotomy between audit and advice' is in some ways 'a false distinction'. Our research evidence shows that helpful inspections that involve professional dialogue may have become a 'bottom up' or 'grass roots' change. Lead inspectors and their teams want to see themselves as partners in a school improvement enterprise and feel that the inspection system should allow them to make a much larger contribution. Primary and secondary heads seem to agree. Politicians and others may worry about 'cosiness' in inspection and may well believe that closer working relationships with schools might blunt inspection's edge and herald the return of the 'blandness' and lack of 'independence and objectivity' of which 'old-style' HMI and LEA inspections had been accused (Burchill, 1991).

Should school self-evaluation play a role?

The registered inspectors' second recommendation from our survey was that the inspection process should provide more encouragement for schools' self-evaluation processes. There were aspects of the inspection criteria which RgIs wanted heads, teachers and governors to judge for themselves and they saw the role of the inspector as more involved in monitoring schools' self-evaluation data and assessing their quality assurance processes and procedures. Surprisingly, the point was not given the same priority by heads (it was identified by only 6 per cent of the primary sample) and was ranked only ninth. MacBeath (1999) envisaged a role for OfSTED inspection in which it sought to 'make itself as redundant as possible' by 'seeking to reinforce the foundations of self-review'. Our research seems to indicate that it is not a thought that has occurred to many headteachers in England. It may be that the influence of MacBeath and others will persuade more English as well as Scottish schools to consider the possibilities of self-evaluation, but it is unusual for academic writers and researchers to have widespread effects on schools or policy-makers. Will heads believe that the considerable efforts required for effective, systematic self-review are in their best interests or could it simply be that schools in England (unlike their Scottish counterparts) are generally uncertain about how self-evaluation should be conducted? One head suggested that OfSTED inspectors should 'deliver self-evaluation packs to the schools'. Indeed, this is now the case as OfSTED has developed materials to accompany their approach to 'self-inspection' or what they prefer (see Chapters 11 and 12) to call 'self-evaluation' (OfSTED, 1998a; DfEE/OfSTED, 1999).

The Select Committee reported that many of its witnesses had put forward the case for school self-evaluation. It concluded that the Inspection Framework should be amended to take account of schools' self-evaluation procedures. By this the Committee meant that schools should be encouraged to develop self-evaluation systems that would themselves be subject to inspection. It did not suggest that the inspection system should take account of the results of school self-evaluation and view them as a contribution to the OfSTED process. This debate has important implications and is explored more fully in Chapter 12. The members endorsed the view (of HMCI for Wales and others) that self-evaluation should not *replace* external inspection. However, this was not a suggestion that was made by either the heads or RgIs who responded to our surveys and, as we have already noted, there is considerable support for the view that an external perspective is needed.

A narrower focus for inspections?

Heads and RgIs gave a similar emphasis to narrowing the focus of inspection. Some heads felt that inspections generally attempted to cover too much ground in the three-, four- or five-day-long inspection visit which is normal in schools. Many were thinking about reinspection when they recommended a concentration on key issues and others believed that the school should be able to determine specific areas of their activity which would be given particular attention. The RgIs felt that inspections would be more effective if they concentrated on the 'essentials' and one respondent, for example, suggested that inspection should 'focus on attainment and progress, teaching and leadership and management as these are the key – especially leadership and management.' Another suggested that there should be 'no pre-OfSTED paperwork for schools' and wanted to see 'a narrower focus for inspection – focusing on the quality of teaching and attainment not on pre-inspection issues.'

Others anticipated the arrangements for the new shorter, 'light touch' or differentiated inspections (see Chapter 11) by suggesting that there should be a narrower focus for effective schools. They generally believed that good schools should have the right to choose at least some of the topics for inspection for themselves. Interesting variations were suggested by RgIs who claimed that the focus of inspections should be less broad to allow them to concentrate on 'national priorities' or on issues that occurred with such frequency that they had become 'generic' and therefore suggested themselves as the natural foci for inspections. National priorities could, it was suggested, be combined with matters identified by the school to provide a sharper focus for future inspections. The Select Committee did not make recommendations about narrowing the focus for inspections in some schools but gave an enthusiastic welcome to the 'light touch' inspections which were introduced for 'successful' schools from January 2000.

A role for the LEA?

The third and the fourth most commonly chosen piece of advice from heads and RgIs respectively was to involve local education authorities in inspection. This sense that LEAs are an under-used asset took a variety of forms and some RgIs (many of whom are still employed by LEAs) made radical suggestions. Most simply wanted the LEA to be represented in inspection teams so that they could contribute to the decision-making process, give the inspection team the benefit of their local knowledge and maintain contact with the school after the inspection team had completed its work. Some RgIs, however, wanted to go further:

> Put more responsibility for inspection back to local level with OfSTED monitoring LEA consistency.

> Give LEAs the responsibility to inspect their own schools. Inspections could be monitored/validated by HMI or OfSTED.

> OfSTED has done its job. LEAs should be charged with the monitoring and inspection function.

Headteachers were no less radical in their suggestions and, like the RgIs, often argued in favour of an LEA/OfSTED 'partnership' in inspection. One in twenty suggested that LEA inspections should replace OfSTED-style inspections. There were suggestions that LEAs should provide more frequent 'interim' inspections which would be used to identify (i) 'areas' for OfSTED to look at in detail and (ii) ineffective schools that would be given full inspections.

The White Paper *Excellence in Schools* (DfEE, 1997a) – much of which became law – defined the role of LEAs as, amongst other things, monitoring school improvement, national tests, parental concerns, target-setting and providing heads with data to compare standards. The chief inspector's annual report (OfSTED, 1999b) was critical of the way that many LEAs discharge their responsibilities (see paragraphs 341 to 347). The fact that OfSTED has been inspecting LEAs since 1998 demonstrates how far the government's view of their relationship with local authorities differs from that of the heads and RgIs. Evans and Penney (1994) studied the effects of the 1988 Education Reform Act in one LEA and pointed out the advantages of inspection by those who are 'knowledgeable and sensitive to the particular institutional circumstances in which teachers work'. These authors concluded, however, that 'interested inspection' was not what the Conservative government wanted to sponsor in 1994. We predicted that the present Labour government would not want to develop a significant role for LEAs either and that the Select Committee would not seek a more significant role for LEAs.

In fact, the Committee did not seem to have engaged in much discussion of the LEAs' role or the mechanisms by which a local perspective might complement or contribute to the outcomes of OfSTED inspection. The Select Committee pointed out that LEA officers have no absolute right to enter schools, but went on to comment: 'However, we believe that effective LEAs will, as a matter of course, use 'drop-in' visits to schools as part of their work in monitoring standards' (House of Commons, 1999a). This is not a change to current arrangements but simply encouragement for one aspect of the limited role that LEAs already play. However, given the current pressure on LEAs (from both OfSTED and the government) to prioritise resources and give emphasis to weak and failing schools, it is debatable whether LEAs will be able to retain 'drop-in' visits.

Reduce the period of notice

The second most frequently chosen piece of advice offered by heads was that the period of notice before an inspection should be reduced. Although one in ten of the RgIs agreed with this advice, it was ranked much lower in the list of their most frequently chosen points. It may have become less of a priority for RgIs because when their survey was being completed not all heads would have been as aware as were the RgIs of OfSTED's decision to reduce the notice period for inspection. Our own research (see Chapter 3) has shown that the pre-inspection period is rarely a time when primary schools are willing to undertake major new development and that a forthcoming inspection can inhibit progress in implementing the school development plan. It is also the period when many teachers feel anxious about the forthcoming inspection and some suffer from stress and 'anticipatory dread' (MORI, 1998; Brimblecombe, Ormston and Shaw, 1995, 1996a; Brunel University CEPPP and Helix Consulting, 1999) and, as we have already argued, the reduction in the notice period explodes the myth that the pre-inspection preparation period can be a catalyst for major school improvements. The Select Committee fully endorsed the heads' and RgIs' recommendations but gave rather different reasons for their decision to reduce the period still further:

> We note that OfSTED has announced, following consultation, that the period of notice given to schools will be between six to ten weeks. We are in favour of reducing the notice period of inspection to the shortest period which is practical. We believe the period of notice should normally be four working weeks. This, we believe, will be welcomed by parents, as it will help to reassure them that the OfSTED inspection team sees their children's school 'as it is' (House of Commons, 1999a, p.64).

In its response to this suggestion, OfSTED state that 'the six to ten weeks notice of inspection to be given from January 2000 is the minimum possible given all that has to take place prior to an inspection' (House of Commons, 1999c, p.23).

Inspectors' qualifications and experience

The registered inspectors were concerned about those among their colleagues who had little or no experience of teaching the National Curriculum or of teaching in the phase which they were inspecting. They complained that the quality of inspection teams was variable, that OfSTED's quality assurance mechanisms needed to be tightened still further and that RgIs' and team members' fitness to carry out inspections should be more rigorously monitored. Primary heads agreed. Like the RgIs they were concerned when they discovered that one of the inspection team lacked primary school experience or had been away from the classroom for many years. The evidence given to the Select Committee led it to conclude that the procedures for assembling inspection teams was in the process of improving and that the change to a six- rather than a four-year inspection cycle would allow contractors to improve the quality of inspection teams still further. The Committee also wanted to see more serving teachers being trained as inspectors and undertaking occasional inspections.

This conclusion, however, seems to have been prompted as much by the desire to make the teaching profession more familiar with the process of inspection as by concerns about the relevance of inspectors' recent experience. The Committee urged governors to encourage teachers to undertake inspections because of the benefits that this was said to bring to the school. We had expected a much stronger statement than this with more critical statements about those inspectors who (i) inspect without having taught the National Curriculum in the phase they are inspecting or (ii) have had no full-time school teaching experience for many years. We also expected a statement about the claims for subject expertise that are made by candidates for training and the development of much more rigorous monitoring of these claims. The Committee did go some way to addressing the concerns of inspectors and heads by asking for improvements to inspector training and to OfSTED's quality assurance mechanisms. However, the point was made in a general way and was not specifically targeted to address the weaknesses that heads and RgIs identified. Contractors can afford to be more discerning in their choice of inspection team members because there is now less inspection work available. This advantage is no replacement for effective quality assurance and could yet prove to be a doubled-edged sword if it helps to increase the rate at which trained OfSTED inspectors decide to become 'inactive'.

We asked our sample of registered inspectors whether they had detected any frequently occurring shortcomings in team inspectors. Almost a half identified common weaknesses and there was a surprising unanimity in the RgIs' responses. Six frequent failings accounted for nearly all of their concerns. They were, in order of priority: (i) inadequacy of writing skills, (ii) inconsistency of judgements, (iii) insufficient knowledge of the Inspection Framework, (iv) professional matters (e.g. teamwork, observing deadlines, time-keeping), (v) lack of subject knowledge and (vi) lack of appropriate school experience. These seem to be important concerns which cast further doubt on the qualities, abilities and experience of some of those who have been permitted to train and practise as OfSTED inspectors. Many will see these shortcomings as a consequence of the replacement of an intensively trained and highly educated inspectorate (HMI) with freelance inspectors of mixed ability and relatively little training.

Registered inspectors wanted members of their inspection teams to provide them with contributions to the final report that were well written, complied with the Inspection Framework (including any recent revisions) and made clear judgements that were firmly rooted in the evidence. However, almost 60 per cent of the RgIs who had detected common weaknesses complained of team inspectors' poor writing skills. They were irritated by team inspectors' 'marked tendency to describe rather than evaluate' and by their 'inability to write coherently'. These shortcomings have unfortunate consequences for lead inspectors who, on occasions, will 'spend days' rewriting the material that has been submitted.

Concern was also expressed about inconsistent judgements and about the inadequacy of some inspectors' knowledge of the Inspection Framework. Over one in ten RgIs complained about team inspectors with insufficient subject knowledge and about those with too little experience of teaching the National Curriculum at the relevant key stage.

One RgI commented that 'our team conduct few inspections and we find it difficult to drop quickly into OfSTED-speak', but heads and governors were dismayed by the distinctive code that has developed within the inspection discourse. A governor from one of our case study primary schools commented:

> It (the school's inspection report) looks pretty devastating. In fact if you look at many areas they say 'good' but often it's done in rather constipated language. Something may be described as 'rarely less than satisfactory'. Initially you think it's not very good because it's the 'less than satisfactory' which you hear. Once you get used to that code, the report is not as bad as it seemed.

The audience for inspection reports is said to be primarily governing bodies and parents and not just teachers (i.e. it is largely a lay audience). Reports should, therefore, be plainly written and easily understood, but not all inspectors, it seems, have been trained to communicate effectively in writing. The Select Committee report commented:

> We are sympathetic to the views expressed to us by school governors that too often inspection reports can obscure the judgements made by inspectors with formulaic language and excessive use of jargon. We recommend OfSTED continue efforts to improve the clarity and usefulness of inspection reports, particularly with regard to the needs of governors (House of Commons, 1999a, paragraph 107).

Contracting and conditions of service

One in five of our sample of registered inspectors identified aspects of their conditions of service as one of their main concerns. Disappointment and anger has been generated by inspectors' perception of low fees, the system of competitive tendering, 'cowboy' contractors and by what they alleged was the sacrifice of quality in order to reduce costs. There were some strongly worded comments:

> The market set up by OfSTED is having a detrimental effect on the quality of inspections. Very low fees are now being paid by contractors. Good team inspectors and RgIs are leaving the market place rapidly and shortly there will be a shortage of team career inspectors. This can only be detrimental to the quality of school inspection overall.

Some RgIs wanted to see the development of an expanded HMI service which would absorb some OfSTED-registered inspectors. The 'marketisation' of inspection, its consequences for RgIs' pay and conditions and its perceived effect in lowering the quality and effectiveness of the process probably accounts for some of the dissatisfaction with the job. The survey asked about RgIs' job satisfaction and revealed that very nearly one-quarter of the sample regarded the job as 'very satisfying' and four in every ten considered their work to be 'satisfying'. Although most registered inspectors obtain considerable job satisfaction, one-third of them do not, declaring that they did not find their work as a RgI 'particularly satisfying' and frequently added critical comments.

The Select Committee provided quite a different perspective on 'cowboy contractors' when it declared itself to be 'in sympathy' with those who felt that they had 'no incentive' to provide high quality training or quality assurance for their inspectors. The dilemma for OfSTED is that support for high quality contractors to the exclusion of those who are unable to achieve high standards would mean a sharp reduction in the number of contractors competing for inspection contracts. This could raise costs as demand exceeded supply and the reduced competition in the market might encourage complacency. The Committee was aware of the likely effects of this limitation of the 'marketisation' of inspection and commented:

> We agree with HM Chief Inspector that it is not desirable to reduce the number of inspection contractors. Nevertheless we expect OfSTED to monitor closely the effects that competition for inspection contracts has on the abilities of contractors to invest in quality assurance measures (House of Commons, 1999a, paragraph 9).

The Committee went on to declare itself to be concerned that inspectors' fees might decline 'to a point where experienced professionals decide not to train as inspectors, or decide to leave the inspectorate, because it is financially not worthwhile.'

This chapter has shown that inspectors and heads share many common concerns, but the advice offered is about relatively minor improvements to the system of OfSTED inspection rather than measures that might radically transform it by introducing the 'quality assurance and quality development' stance of much of the rest of Europe. The Parliamentary Select Committee's advice is even more conservative. There is no desire to provide the kind of role for self-evaluation advocated by MacBeath (1999) and others, and no wish to restore HMIs' or LEAs' influence in schools. Nor did the Committee want inspectors to become involved with schools or to pursue school improvement directly. The report declares: 'The relationship between inspectors and school staff is the most important factor in the success of the inspection' (paragraph 102) and advocates 'professional dialogue between inspectors and staff' (paragraph 100). Some school staff might assume that this means friendly relationships and a desire to provide senior managers with 'free consultancy', but this would be a misunderstanding. Professional dialogue is 'to afford the opportunities for teachers to see clearly how inspectors have reached their judgements' and 'the all-important relationships should ensure that the "optimal tension" exists: the relationship should be neither too stressful nor too close' (paragraph 79). Inspection is about accountability but includes an invitation to schools to use the experience, if they can, to plan for improvements. Heads, inspectors and the Select

Committee recognised this. Those who believe that OfSTED inspection is, in significant ways, about school improvement or who have gained the impression that it is an unpopular process on the verge of major change have misjudged the climate of national opinion. There seems to be little appetite for radical changes.

Professional issues for discussion

- Of the suggestions recommended by heads and inspectors, which relate to inspection's accountability function and which to school improvement?
- Does the Select Committee have a clear view regarding the main purpose of inspection?
- Why do so few schools choose to employ inspectors in post-inspection work? Is it simply a question of cost or are other factors important?
- How can we ensure that school self-evaluation is not a soft option and that it is as least as rigorous as inspection?

9

'Failing' schools and the inner city

One of the possible outcomes of an OfSTED inspection is the decision that a school is 'failing' or is likely to fail to provide an acceptable standard of education. Such schools are said to be 'in need of special measures'. Our Nuffield Foundation funded research projects were never intended to be studies of 'failing' schools; in fact we argued strongly that what was needed were studies of the effects of inspection on *all* schools and especially those that might be described as 'average' or 'typical'. As might be expected in a national study of inspection, some failing and seriously weak schools were found in our samples and indeed such examples were included in the case studies. It was felt necessary, however, in a study of the impact of OfSTED inspections, to provide a brief summary of what we know about schools in special measures. This in turn leads us to ask a series of questions about the inspection of schools located in the inner cities and those serving socially and economically disadvantaged communities. Why is it, for example, that so many 'failing' schools are found in such areas? Only one in 100 schools with a high proportion of socially disadvantaged children receive 'very good' inspection reports compared with one in five of those with only a small proportion. How are inspection judgements made on inner-city schools? Are they equitable and likely to help inner-city schools to improve the quality of education they offer? We do not claim to have the answers to such questions but feel it is important to raise the issues.

'Failing' schools and those with serious weaknesses

In inspecting a school, registered inspectors (RgIs) and their teams will use the OfSTED framework to make judgements about the standard of education the school provides. A school may be deemed 'to be in need of special measures' or 'failing' if there is evidence of the following:

- low attainment and poor progress
- regular disruptive behaviour
- harassment
- poor attendance or high levels of truancy
- a high proportion of unsatisfactory teaching
- failure to deliver the National Curriculum
- pupils at physical or emotional risk within the school community
- poor relationships between staff and pupils
- ineffective management, including the governing body
- significant loss of confidence in the headteacher
- low morale and high turnover in staff
- poor management of resources or ineffective use of them
- poor value for money.

Not all of these factors need to be present for a school to become subject to special measures. In fact the most consistent factors found in failing schools are the underachievement of pupils, a high proportion of unsatisfactory teaching and ineffective leadership and management causing the school to fail to provide satisfactory value for money (OfSTED, 1997b; OfSTED, 1999b). However, before the school is placed on the special measures register, the inspectors' decision has to be corroborated by Her Majesty's Inspectorate (HMI) who will visit the school, usually within a few weeks after the initial inspection. In all but a very small number of cases the inspectors' original decision has been ratified and the need for special measures confirmed. About six months later, HMI will visit again for the first of their termly monitoring visits. During these visits, HMI 'inspect classroom practice to evaluate standards of attainment, the progress being made by pupils and the quality of education being provided, and assess the progress the school is making to address the key issues' (OfSTED, 1999a, p.1). These visits will continue until the school is seen as providing an acceptable standard of education and special measures are removed.

The inspectors or HMI may decide that a school is not failing but does have 'serious weaknesses'. As with a failing school, the factors that lead to such a judgement would include: unsatisfactory standards, particularly in the core subjects, poor teaching (in more than 25 per cent of lessons), concerns about pupil behaviour and relationships, ineffective management, poor value for money, low attendance and a high number of pupil exclusions. Serious-weakness schools would not be seen as sufficiently poor to warrant being labelled 'failing'. If the school is deemed to have 'serious weaknesses' this is clearly stated in the inspection report, so the headteacher, governing body and parents are aware of the situation. The resulting post-OfSTED action plan will be given particular scrutiny and a school with 'serious weaknesses' can expect a visit from HMI within six months to a year. It is possible for such a school to be reclassified as in need of special measures if HMI subsequently form the opinion that sufficient progress has not been made.

Not many schools fall into either of these categories. At the end of the first inspection cycle, about 2 to 3 per cent of primary and secondary schools and 8 per cent of special schools were found to require special measures. In addition, about one school in ten has been identified as having serious weaknesses. Between September 1993, when inspections first commenced, and July 1998 when all schools had been inspected at least once, just over 700 schools were identified as in need of special measures. By the end of the 1998–99 school year, over 250 schools had been removed from the special measures register. The time taken before the school is 'turned round' and is judged to be offering an acceptable standard of education varies. In 1999 it took 17 months on average for a school to be removed from the special measures register compared with 25 months in 1997. The shortest period has been one year after the date of the initial inspection. It is generally expected that schools will be removed from the register after two years although some have taken longer because of the complex nature of the problems to be resolved. The government announced in 1997 that schools that fail to re-move themselves from the register 'within a two-year period' will be closed and may be reopened with new names and given 'a fresh start'. This has occurred in over 50 cases.

Some initial analyses of 'failing' schools, conducted by government agencies, outlined their main features (DfEE, 1996; TTA, 1995; DfE/OfSTED, 1995b; Stark, 1998), while more recently OfSTED have published accounts of how special measures have helped schools to improve (OfSTED, 1997b; 1999a). Other studies of 'failing', ineffective and dysfunctional schools, conducted by LEAs and educational researchers, are also available (e.g. Reynolds, 1996; Riley, 1996; Stoll and Myers, 1998; Wilcox and Gray, 1996; Aris, Davies and Johnson, 1998; Biott and Gulson, 1999; Scanlon, 1999) along with numerous accounts in the educational press of schools which have been removed from the special measures register (e.g. Sharron, 1996; Salmon, 1997). The DfEE commissioned the International School Effectiveness and Improvement Centre (ISEIC) at the Institute of Education, University of London, to produce case studies of several schools that no longer require special measures. The first of these studies was published in 1997 (DfEE, 1997c).

The most recent example of this growing body of literature on 'failing' schools is the OfSTED publication *Lessons Learned from Special Measures*. This report, based on the experiences of the first 250 schools to be removed from special measures, concludes that 'no single solution will serve as a panacea to remedy all the ills that befall schools' (OfSTED, 1999a, p.2) and it is careful to point out that there are many ways to secure improvement, noting that strategies that work in some schools will not necessarily work in others. However, the report does attempt to describe the improvement strategies that HMI have seen successfully working and it 'traces the path of the journey, from the initial judgement of failure to the joy of success when special measures are removed' (p.2).

The key factors that HMI identify in assisting special measures schools to improve form the basis of each section of the report. These factors are discussed (with examples) under the following headings:

- 'Getting started' (e.g. quickly coming to terms with feelings of distress, shock and anger when special measures are applied; involving all stakeholders in the construction and implementation of the action plan)
- 'A better deal for pupils' (e.g. celebrating pupils' achievements; raising esteem; establishing ways to check standards)
- 'Promoting positive attitudes' (e.g. addressing inappropriate behaviour; finding ways to encourage attendance and punctuality)
- 'The way ahead for teachers and support staff' (e.g. focusing on learning objectives; a common approach to planning; agreeing a common assessment policy)
- 'The role of co-ordinators and heads of department' (e.g. ensuring schemes of work and plans are in place; evaluating the department's effectiveness; contributing to a team approach to addressing the school's problems)
- 'Headteachers and senior managers moving forward' (e.g. providing leadership; focusing on achievement; offering guidance about pedagogy; analysing performance data; monitoring and evaluating teaching to guide decisions; adjusting the school's priorities in the light of external monitors' findings)
- 'Governors taking the lead' (e.g. securing the services of an effective head; becoming involved in the work of the school; questioning staff about decisions; monitoring, particularly progress on the action plan; managing staff competence procedures)
- 'Moving forward with parents' (e.g. involving parents and encouraging partnerships)
- 'Making full use of external support' (e.g. ensuring LEA officers provide a balance of advice, training and monitoring; employing consultants for advice; using ideas developed elsewhere)
- 'Coming out of special measures and moving on' (e.g. maintaining an improvement momentum; establishing a plan for phased withdrawal of support to ensure self-sufficiency). (Adapted from OfSTED, 1999a, pp.4–5.)

The report states that there are no magic solutions and that ultimately:

> Each school must find its own route along the road to improvement and make its own critical evaluation of its progress. If the leaders realise they are not making progress, the school may need to alter its strategies. The formal monitoring by HMI and further monitoring by the headteacher, the senior management team, heads of department, co-ordinators, governors, the local education authority or consultants should provide the evidence necessary to evaluate the school's performance (OfSTED, 1999a, p.2).

Schools in special measures are found in all phases of education (primary and secondary), although special schools have been found to have a higher rate of failure (7–8 per cent) than other schools (2–3 per cent). In *From Failure to Success*, OfSTED states that special-measures schools 'range from inner-city secondary and primary schools to rural village schools' (OfSTED, 1997b, p.4), noting that many serve pupils from areas with high levels of deprivation. The report goes on to comment that:

> This is not an excuse for failing to educate pupils properly because there can be no valid reason for not providing all young people with an acceptable quality of education. OfSTED inspections show clearly that schools serving similar areas often perform very differently; some well and some poorly (OfSTED, 1997b, p.4).

and:

> Whether a school is small or large, urban or rural, primary, secondary or special, nothing can substitute for good quality teaching and good leadership (ibid., p.5).

It does appear, however, that a disproportionate number of 'failing' schools are located in the inner city and in areas of social and economic disadvantage. The chief inspector's annual report notes that just over one-third of primary schools in special measures and about one-half of secondary schools had intakes 'with high levels of disadvantage in and around large cities' (OfSTED, 1999b, p.54). This fact raises a number of interesting questions about inspectors' judgements of such schools.

Poverty is no excuse

Before examining the judgements made on inner-city schools, we need to explore some wider issues of the impact of disadvantage on educational performance. Byers (1997) – at that time an education minister – said that 'poverty is no excuse' for educational failure. Education is not seeking excuses but poverty does appear to be consistently correlated with lower educational achievement. There is evidence to support the view that social disadvantage plays a part in poor educational attainment (Mortimore and Whitty, 1999). The best predictor of attainment at any age is prior attainment. Social factors appear to be much less powerful once previous attainment is taken into account. It may be this finding which has led to the mistaken conclusion that social disadvantage is of little importance. It seems highly likely that social disadvantage *in the early years* will have an effect on early attainment. Continuing social disadvantage, and poor health, will continue to depress attainment, but its impact may be masked by the lower levels of prior attainment.

It is very clear from many studies that children living in disadvantaged areas suffer a range of adverse influences: family poverty, poor housing, racism, and poor physical and mental health (Ouston, 1999). The recent research of Davis *et al.* (forthcoming) investigated the experiences of inner-city families which seem to have direct implications for children's progress at school. As might be expected, the sample included a high proportion of children from single parent, low income and unemployed families, and from ethnic minority backgrounds. There were very low levels of home ownership. Seventy-two per cent of children had at least one significant psychosocial problem and 37 per cent had three or more. These varied according to age: in the 0–4 age group the most common was 'disruptive attention-seeking behaviour' (23 per cent); 5–10 years, 'general anxiety' (19 per cent); 11–13 years, 'temper control' (28 per cent); and, in the 14–16 age group, 'crime' (29 per cent).

Eighty-six per cent of the sample were exposed to at least one family risk factor and 51 per cent experienced three or more. The most frequent were maternal mental health problems (34 per cent) and housing problems (34 per cent); 20 per cent of mothers felt lacking in external social support. Fathers, too, experienced problems: 19 per cent had mental health problems, and the same proportion had chronic physical health problems or had been in trouble with the police. Of both mothers and fathers, 11 per cent had lived away from home as children because of family problems. Twenty-six per cent of children had experienced significant bereavements. Only 10 per cent of children had not experienced significant psychosocial problems and were free from family risk factors.

There were clear relationships between the number of problems and the number of risk factors experienced. Conversely, 28 per cent of children had no significant psychosocial problems, and as a group experienced far fewer family risk factors than others. These data show very clearly the stresses that young people and their families in this inner-city area suffer and the demands that these will make on local schools. In such circumstances, it is not surprising that there is often a lack of support from parents for the school's efforts to reduce truancy, ensure that homework is completed on time and that pupils behave well in school.

Evidence of rising standards against a background of factors that are hampering schools' efforts to improve, deserve to be recognised. However, as Law and Glover (1999) comment in their discussion of the inspection of inner-city schools, 'the use of tightly defined and *nationally* developed OfSTED criteria for what is satisfactory or better still inhibits the potential for praise' (p.162). The authors go on to explain that this reluctance to recognise success persists even when value-added measures suggest that the school's achievements deserve recognition or the school can demonstrate that it has improved considerably since the previous inspection.

Judgements of inner-city schools

This section explores how inspection judgements are made of inner-city schools, whether they are equitable and whether they are likely to help schools improve the quality of education they offer their pupils. There are essentially two questions about whether we should:

- expect the same levels of achievement in inner-city schools as from those in the more affluent suburbs, and,
- judge inner-city schools by the same criteria as others. Is it right that 'poverty is no excuse' or that 'education cannot compensate for society' (Bernstein, 1970)?

Throughout the assessment of inner-city schools there is a tension between judgements based on schools' actual achievements and those that allow for context by taking account of benchmark and 'value-added' data. There are serious concerns about OfSTED's judgements of inner-city schools, yet these are crucial in an education culture where, as we have shown, performance indicators and inspection findings have such 'high stakes'.

First, there is a clear relationship between schools' free school meals entitlement (FSM) and the judgements made by OfSTED inspectors. Considering 'comprehensive' schools only, on four summary measures: 'standards achieved by pupils', 'quality of education', 'the school's climate', and 'management and efficiency', it is clear that socially disadvantaged schools receive worse inspection judgements. Table 9.1 gives the percentage of schools in each group given a 'very good grade' by inspectors. Table 9.2 shows the percentage where 'substantial improvement is required'. The data shown in Tables 9.1 and 9.2 are taken from OfSTED (OfSTED,1999c, p.9). Negative judgements are made much more frequently in schools serving disadvantaged families. Interestingly, OfSTED have rejected this interpretation (Cassidy, 1999) although these data have come directly from an OfSTED publication and are readily available. Borchers (1999) asked why this relationship should exist:

Table 9.1 Percentage of 'comprehensive' schools judged 'very good'

% Free school meals ⇒	0–5%	5–9%	9–13%	13–21%	21–35%	35%+
Standards	56	40	17	10	4	1
Quality	34	25	10	16	8	4
Climate	77	70	51	36	29	19
Management and efficiency	53	45	28	26	22	14

Table 9.2 Percentage of 'comprehensive' schools where 'substantial improvement is required'

% Free school meals ⇒	0–5%	5–9%	9–13%	13–21%	21–35%	35%+
Standards	2	2	3	6	16	39
Quality	3	3	3	6	11	18
Climate	0	1	2	4	7	16
Management and efficiency	1	4	5	5	10	15

> Is it because poorer areas have weak teachers and incompetent managers, or is it because the OfSTED system makes it almost inevitable that schools in deprived areas will get poor reports? (p.19).

This is a serious issue which OfSTED seems disinclined to examine. The difficulties of teaching in inner cities and the impact of social disadvantage on student achievement are rarely denied, but should OfSTED be compounding the difficulties of these schools by operating an inspection system which takes no account of them?

Within the OfSTED school inspection methodology, absolute and relative measures are both used: school performance is compared with national norms, and with relative measures. This may provide a confusing picture for inner-city schools where they are doing very poorly compared to national averages, and, at the same time, very well compared to 'similar' schools. OfSTED judgements of the quality of teaching and learning, however, are normally expected to be absolute (i.e. the criteria are common across all schools), although it is not clear how this expectation is realised in practice. This again raises a question which underlies the whole of the section of this chapter in different forms: does fair assessment of schools require us to use the same criteria, or to take account of their context?

Benchmark data

The use of benchmark data is an attempt to 'compare like with like', that is, to take account of school context (see Fidler, 1999 and Chapter 10). The Qualifications and Curriculum Authority (QCA) publishes Key Stage test and GCSE results grouped according to the proportion of children in each school entitled to free school meals (used as a proxy measure for poverty and social disadvantage). Given that it is widely accepted that social disadvantage is related to lower levels of attainment, it has been a constant source of irritation to inner-city schools that the QCA benchmark data group all schools with over 35 per cent free school meals together. Schools reasonably ask how, if they have, say, 65 per cent of their students eligible to receive free meals, they can be considered 'similar' to those with 35 per cent. There are over 450 secondary schools in this 35%+ category, quite enough to provide a more finely graded analysis. The current benchmarks are unfair to inner-city schools; there is no reason why QCA could not publish a fairer set of comparisons for schools serving socially disadvantaged areas.[1] The DfEE expects to resolve these problems in the future with the development of a national value-added database.

Value-added measures

It has been argued for many years that judging schools on their actual test and examination results is unhelpful and unfair and that the ideal is to use

---

1. OfSTED and QCA have recently responded to this concern and now group schools in a greater number of FSM entitlement categories.

'value-added' measures, which take into account differences in intake. Recent analyses have demonstrated, however, that after taking account of the characteristics of students admitted to a school, the majority of schools cannot be distinguished from each other (Croxford and Cowie, 1996; Goldstein and Spiegelhalter, 1996). Another issue concerns the extent to which such analyses take full account of intake characteristics. Schagen (1999) explored the outcomes of different approaches to value-added analysis of the examination results of 220 secondary schools. He showed that controlling for pupil variables (such as prior attainment) resulted in schools with lower absolute performance also having lower 'value-added' performance. When a range of factors relating to school characteristics (having a sixth form, the catchment area, staff turnover, parental attendance at meetings, proportion of students eligible for free school meals, proportion of students with SEN) were included in the calculations, 'only a small minority (of schools) remain significantly higher or lower than would be expected' (Schagen,1999, p.9). To sum up, value-added analyses using school-level data which include a wide range of measures demonstrate the powerful impact of individual and context factors on achievement, but if inadequate numbers of background factors are included these methods disadvantage those schools serving disadvantaged families.

As noted above, the DfEE is planning to establish a national database, operational by January 2002, which will include information on all pupils (House of Commons, 1999c, p.4). In the same document OfSTED write, 'We want to move very quickly to value-added measures based on prior attainment which will remove the need for comparisons to be made on the basis of free school meals data' (p.29). If the analyses are undertaken at the level of the individual pupil, research suggests that the majority of schools will not differ from one another. If the analyses are at school level, then disadvantaged schools will continue to be disadvantaged.

Conclusion

Inspectors' judgements of inner-city schools and those serving disadvantaged communities clearly remain a complex and contested area. A deputy head from an inner-city school who had carried out an analysis of more than two years of statistics from OfSTED inspection reports concluded:

> The figures show that most schools in challenging socio-economic environments appear to be doomed to be damned by reports which are incapable of recognising teaching effort, quality, competence, commitment and resilience (Cassidy, 1999).

It is suggested that rather than concluding that inner-city schools are full of weak teachers, poor managers and dismal academic climates, 'an alternative explanation might be that the very structure and processes of OfSTED inspections makes it almost inevitable that such schools will receive poor reports' (Cassidy, 1999). This is an explanation that OfSTED disagrees with but, as earlier noted, seems reluctant to investigate further.

The chief inspector has pointed out that 'The rich do not, however, have a monopoly on intelligence and poverty can be no excuse for school failure' (OfSTED, 1999b, p.17). However, low levels of pupil performance do not necessarily indicate poor teaching. Pupils from deprived backgrounds, for reasons that are often beyond the control of teachers, are more demanding to teach. Inspectors are able to recognise good teaching but it is difficult to teach well in the conditions that are found in many inner-city schools. It is also well known that inner-city schools frequently experience difficulties in recruiting and retaining teachers. Howson (1999) reports that the highest rates of vacancies in both primary and secondary schools are in London and that in January 1999 there were 544 primary vacancies (41 per cent of the national total) and 320 secondary vacancies (33 per cent of the national total).

Whether future value-added analyses, performance data more accurately linked to FSM percentages and individual pupil identifier numbers will make for fairer judgements of inner-city schools remains to be seen. We know that some schools do succeed 'against the odds' (National Commission of Education, 1995; OfSTED, 1999b). The question still remains, however, whether the system of inspection, as currently operating, is judging inner-city schools fairly and helping to enhance the quality of education they provide.

Professional issues for discussion

- An inner-city school is harshly judged and its report contains a large number of substantial key issues. The school's action on the KIs leads eventually to some significant improvements. Is this situation a matter for concern?
- How should teachers in inner-city schools think about their pupils? Should they adopt the stance 'poverty is no excuse' or 'poverty *is* an excuse'?
- Imagine you are a parent governor in a school that has been put into special measures. What feelings would you have? How would you react? What do you think you might be saying at the next meeting of the governing body? Now imagine you are a teacher governor. How might this change your answers to any of these questions?

10

Assisted school self-review in Victoria, Australia

This chapter examines the potential of assisted self-review as an aid to school improvement. There is a particular focus on the value of comparative data on school processes and outcomes as a contribution to the review process.

There have been some moves over recent years by LEAs and by OfSTED to provide schools with data sets from other comparable schools. These have generally consisted of data which were collected for other purposes but which schools might find useful. There has been little activity in collecting specific new data on either process or outcomes.

The school review process in Victoria, Australia, involves the collection of data about the curriculum and student performance, staff opinions, parental views and, in the future, students' views. This data collection uses common instruments in each school so that the results can be compared with similar results from all schools and also 'like schools'. These data are collected and examined by school staff for their implications for the school's operation. Any need for changes is prioritised and incorporated in the school's future planning.

The Victorian experience will be briefly described before the potential for the use of comparative data is considered for schools in England and Wales as a component of a school review process.

Benchmarking and comparative data collection

There is a good deal of confusion about the meaning of the term benchmarking. Benchmarking is sometimes used loosely in education to mean the comparison of data sets as, for example, when schools in areas with similar socio-economic characteristics are compared on a variety of attainment outcomes, truancy rates, exclusions and so forth. This use of the word 'benchmarking' to mean the collection of data for purposes of comparison loses an important conceptual distinction. Comparative data can be used as a benchmark for performance but we prefer to restrict the use of 'benchmarking' to the identification of best practice in another organisation and its replication since this is the managerial use of the term (Camp, 1996). Therefore in this chapter comparative data collection (CDC) will be the phrase used for collecting and comparing data sets or 'benchmarks', whereas 'benchmarking' would involve the identification of a high performing partner school (or schools) and the study of its operating processes.

The transformation of inputs into outputs by a process can be represented in a simple systems model as shown in Figure 10.1. There are a range of inputs such as resources and the skills of teachers but the main focus here is on the changes to children brought about by the educational process.

Figure 10.1 Simple systems model showing the transformation of inputs into outputs

In the case of a school, one input would represent children with an initial state of knowledge and the corresponding output would include the same children with increased knowledge. The processes which had occurred in school would include teaching and the provision of other learning opportunities. If two schools are compared which have similar inputs then the superior performing school is the one which has higher outputs. However, while this comparison might give some guide as to the level of output which could be obtained, it gives little help as regards obtaining higher outputs. A study of the teaching and learning processes in the higher performing school, however, should give some indication as to how the higher outputs are obtained.

The benchmarking technique involves identifying superior performance in another organisation, discovering how that organisation achieves its superior performance and replicating the superior performance in the home organisation. It is a form of 'management borrowing'. Benchmarking has a number of forms but an essential element in the technique is the study of one or more other organisation's processes in order to transplant and replicate them. It is a very valuable technique which is covered in more detail elsewhere (Fidler, 1999). Here the specific focus is on the collection and comparison of (benchmark) data (CDC) but without contact with other organisations (benchmarking).

Schools in England and Wales currently receive information which allows them to compare their pupils' scores on a range of outcome measures with those from other schools. The principal outcome measures are Key Stage results in the National Curriculum and external examinations (GCSE and 'A' level). In addition to the comparable results from all other schools of the same type, more precise comparisons are possible with schools which have similar student characteristics. This is fairly crude since the proportion of children entitled to free school meals (FSM) is used as a measure of social deprivation. Thus a school can compare the performance of its children with those in schools with about the same proportion of entitlement to free school meals (see Chapter 9).

Although comparisons of outcomes of this kind are of some value, they provide very little insight into possible reasons for performance differences. This is because they provide no information on school processes – teaching and learning, school decision-making and resource deployment, for example. Knowing something of these internal processes in schools which have more successful outcomes could help focus investigations in those schools which aim to improve their performance.

A further weakness of our system is that the data do not provide feedback from the school's clients about the school's performance. This is particularly unfortunate when parents have some choice of school to which to send their children. The urgency of action to improve results may differ according to circumstances, as Figure 10.2 illustrates.

		Parental perceptions	
		Poor	Good
School performance	Poor	Urgent need to improve results if pupil numbers are not to fall	Results need to be improved before parental perceptions change
	Good	The school's good results need to be promoted in the community	The good results need to be maintained

Figure 10.2   The influence of parental perceptions on the urgency of the need to improve school performance

In the last few years many LEAs have been providing schools with data which give some insight into the internal workings of schools. These data were almost invariably collected for other reasons but they were collected on a standardised form and so could be fed back to schools together with comparative figures from other schools in the LEA or schools with particular characteristics, e.g. same size, same proportion of free school meals, same geographic area. This includes, in addition to financial data, such data as:

- staffing – distribution of responsibility points, number of part-time/full-time staff, pupil–teacher ratio, number and types of teaching support staff, teacher turnover
- pupils – number of statements of special education need, gender balance of pupils, number of exclusions, participation in non-compulsory schooling
- curriculum and teaching – length of taught week, average class size, vocational courses, teacher contact ratio.

Inspections conducted according to the OfSTED framework provide schools with a range of information on a comparative basis. This includes both factual information and judgemental assessments of the quality of education provided by the school; the educational standards achieved by pupils; its spiritual, social, moral and cultural development; and the efficiency with which resources are managed (see Chapter 2).

However, this information is only provided once every four to six years. While PANDA (performance and assessment) reports are sent to schools annually, these give the current examination and test results but merely repeat the gradings for the four areas listed above from the last inspection. These grades are accompanied by comparison grades for all schools and for schools in a broad band which includes the school's proportion of FSM entitlement. Thus a school might be told that its management and efficiency required some improvement and that this was the case for 27 per cent of all schools and 29 per cent of schools in a band with 23–49 per cent of children entitled to free meals.

These judgements depend upon the Inspection Framework and the inspectors making the judgements. This has two disadvantages. Firstly, the Framework is primarily an accountability framework rather than one compiled to be helpful to a school for improvement purposes and so, although it reports on the situation at the time, there is little process information which could be helpful for the process of change. The second disadvantage is that the judgements are only as good as the inspectors and their experience. Where these are contested by teachers they do not provide a basis for an agreed benchmark on which to base change.

A further issue concerned with OfSTED inspections is that they are imposed on schools. They are standardised on a common framework but they include hardly any comparative data from similar schools on process factors. It should be pointed out that inspection reports do provide an indirect way of obtaining process data. As the reports are publicly available on the Internet it is possible to identify schools which have received a good report on a particular aspect of their performance. Inspection reports for such schools can be searched for useful process data which give insights into how these schools obtain such good results. They also provide details such as addresses and phone numbers to make contact with the schools to enable a discussion of their processes or visits to observe them in action.[1]

Other major concerns, as noted earlier, are that inspection is not tailored to the school and its specific intentions, and that the OfSTED approach may come to constitute an orthodoxy to which schools and governing bodies may feel they should comply. This may reduce the innovative capacity of teachers and schools.

Comparative data collection, inspections and school improvement

The requirements for school improvement are fivefold:

- knowledge of what to improve
- knowledge of how to improve
- motivation to engage in improvement
- resources and know-how to facilitate improvement
- feedback on the progress of improvement efforts.

Comparative data collection and assisted self-review can help with each of these requirements. They are part of a move towards evidence-based practice. This recognises that decisions should be informed by systematically collected evidence rather than by relying on general impressions, hunches and professional experience alone. Professional judgement is still essential, however, to interpret the evidence.

An advantage of quantitative and qualitative data as elements of the review process is that these are more neutral than a summary judgement by an inspector. The data are neutral, although what data have been collected and how they are analysed involve judgemental decisions. The data require interpretation, but different individuals may come to different conclusions about the implications of the same data. This can provide a useful spur to discussion and, moreover, discussion based on evidence. Often any interpretation will be ambiguous and further investigation will be needed to clarify the findings. However, by engaging personally in the collection and interpretation of the data, individuals are likely to have a greater stake in the outcomes of the process. Such activities incline people to be curious and ask questions. A danger of this approach, of course, is 'analysis-paralysis'. Ever-increasing amounts of energy can be devoted to investigations which often reveal more and more complexity. Meanwhile children are being taught and move through their school career and have only the one opportunity to experience good teaching at each phase of their schooling. Thus a balance is needed between investigation, planning and action. Improvement requires action as well as investigation.

The process of data collection by schools can be contrasted with the process of OfSTED inspection where the outcome of the experience is a summary judgement written by a lead inspector. Where this is well informed, supported with evidence, and where the inspector making the assessment is known to have sound judgement based on extensive experience, then there is every reason to trust the conclusion.

Where this points to a need for action and this is accepted by staff in a school, the important issues are concerned with motivation, knowledge of how to improve, etc. Where, however, any of the previous assumptions are in doubt – evidence, informed judgement – then the scope for staff to reject the judgement and to legitimate their rejection is much increased. There are further issues of concern which include the agenda being set by the OfSTED Inspection Framework rather than the school and the possibilities of misunderstanding the nature of the required improvements if the formulation of any of the key issues for action by inspectors is less than clear (see Chapter 5).

This is not to argue that an agenda set by a school is necessarily better than one set by OfSTED, but it is likely that both parties need to make an input if a school is to be judged both according to national standards and against its own specific intentions.

A summary table (Table 10.1) compares the effects of inspection and self-review on each of the earlier noted five requirements for school improvement.

Table 10.1 Comparison of self-review and inspection on the five requirements for school improvement

Requirement	OfSTED inspection	Self-review
Knowledge of what to improve	Key areas for action within framework identified by inspectors	Discovered by staff as a result of collecting data and comparing it with that from other schools
Knowledge of how to improve	None	Original data may give indications and further data can be collected
Motivation to engage in improvements	Professional duty and coercion of next inspection	Ownership of problem and next year's data possibly reiterating a need for action if nothing is done
Resources to facilitate improvement	Value for money judgement on existing resources and further resources released by an acceptable action plan	Comparative financial data on existing spending and further resources released by an acceptable action plan
Feedback on the progress of improvement efforts	Summative judgement in the next inspection cycle	Collection of further formative and summative data

Assisted self-review in Australia

The State of Victoria in Australia examined approaches to school account-ability in other countries and devised a school review procedure in the early 1990s which tries to balance the needs of accountability and school develop-ment. It requires schools to collect considerable quantities of data which are then compared with data from similar schools. However, this review pro-cedure is embedded in an educational system which has particular charac-teristics. Thus any account of how the review process works and its successes needs to be situational and contingent upon formal requirements and prevailing attitudes and norms in the system. The review process could not just be applied to a different educational system without modification since the assumptions about schools and by schools are not the same as in England although there are a number of similarities.

In many ways Victoria and England are moving in opposite directions as regards self-management. Victoria has devised a self-governing regime for the future which is closer to the grant maintained status which has just been abandoned in England. England appears to be moving to a greater degree of central prescription.

The context will be briefly described before the review process is assessed for its potential for schools in England. One of the authors (Brian Fidler) recently visited Victoria and gives his thoughts on the process as he ob-served it and from documentary evidence.

Context

Australia is a federation of states and territories but constitutionally the states have responsibility for education. Thus states and territories have different accountability structures for schools. Victoria has set up a Curricu-lum and Standards Framework (CSF) which each school is expected to follow. The progress of students is assessed only by teachers although there are voluntary tests for Years 3, 5, 7 and 9 and a school-leaving examination at age 18 which is state moderated. Each school has a school council mainly composed of parents but this has much less power than governing bodies in England and Wales.

Although there is parental preference of school, observation and discussion in schools suggest that market mechanisms and school independence are rather low key compared to direction from the state and a strong professional ethos. For example, the performance-related pay of each head or principal is negotiated with education department officers, and the school's charter or three-year plan has to reflect one priority of the education department. Each charter has to be approved by the state education department. When the purposes of education were discussed (with BF), intrinsic values were more likely to be raised than extrinsic ones and em-ployers were rarely mentioned.

Although there has been financial delegation, staffing flexibility is limited and union pressure, by the standards of England, is strong. Schools can apply to accept responsibility for staffing but this takes the current teacher establishment as fixed. Only new staff are affected.

The review process operates in the two-thirds of schools in Victoria which are government schools. This involves some 1,300 primary schools and almost 300 secondary schools (Gurr, 1999).

Accountability and school reviews

The three elements recently introduced into the accountability framework for Victoria's schools (Office of Review, 1997) are:

- school charter
- school annual report
- triennial school review.

These are inter-related as Figure 10.3 shows.

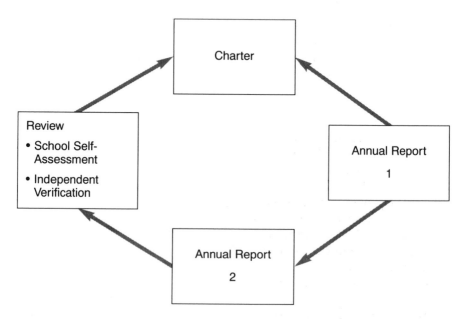

Figure 10.3   The accountability framework

The 'school charter' involves a public declaration of priorities for the following three years. The review process examines the school's progress in fulfilling these charter aims. Each school draws up its charter of goals for a three-year period and reports on progress each year for the first two years.

The triennial review incorporates the two previous annual reports and assesses the degree to which charter goals have been accomplished and identifies additional areas for improvement. This review informs the formulation of a new charter for the next three years. The triennial review has two phases – internal school self-assessment followed by external verification.

The process is overseen by a section of the State Education Department called the Office of Review. This has set up contracts for verification of the school self-assessment as part of the triennial school review process. Verification checks that appropriate data have been collected and analysed, that appropriate inferences have been made and that suitable action is planned. The verifier role is contracted to ten agencies (five universities and five other groups). The verification task for an individual school, including the review meeting, is carried out by one person called the verifier or reviewer.

The review meeting includes the principal and president of the school council and such others as the school chooses to include. For primary schools this may include the vice-principal and others while in secondary schools, specialists are likely to be brought in for part of the meeting. These are likely to be leading teachers and the vice-principals. The review meeting works through sections of the triennial report. This takes the form of a dialogue where school representatives make brief presentations on the data, their interpretation of it and any proposed actions, and the reviewer asks questions, volunteers information and offers advice about priorities. The reviewer is able to gauge the acceptability of some recommendations to the school personnel.

The outcome will lead to priorities for the next school charter as some new developmental activities emerge and other priorities are maintained.

School charter

Since the mid-1990s each school in consultation with parents has formulated a 'charter' which is made public and which makes commitments for three years in a restricted range of priorities. These priorities are chosen within State guidelines. The charter contains statements on the school profile or context; the school's goals which identify key improvement areas including priorities and improvement foci and which identify intended outcomes; and codes of practice of student behaviour and parental support.

Goals are expected to be developed in the following areas:

- curriculum
- educational environment
- people management
- management of financial and physical resources.

Two areas are expected to be covered in curriculum goals – student learning outcomes and curriculum provision.

Self-assessment

As a contribution to school and system accountability, progress on these charter priorities and a number of other indicators are reported to parents each year. In some cases the indicators involve the presentation of statistical data for students in terms of their:

- achievement in external assessment
- achievement as assessed against the Curriculum and Standards Framework
- destinations
- attendance
- welfare

and for staff, in terms of:

- professional development activities
- absence

and for the school:

- curriculum performance (subjects and courses offered)

while in other areas the results of survey instruments administered to different groups are displayed:

- parental satisfaction
- staff opinion.

One of the most interesting aspects of data collection is that obtained from a staff survey. From development work in Victoria it is claimed that 14 components of effective staff management have been identified and these are assessed in a set of questions in the staff survey. This survey is only designed for teaching staff. The components are shown in Table 10.2.

The first five components are reported each year (in responses to 24 statements) while all 14 are covered only in a full staff survey. Variables 1–11 have a positive scale while 12–14 have a negative scale.

The morale variable reports the general feeling in the school about the extent of 'energy, enthusiasm and pride' among staff while distress assesses 'anxiety, depression and frustration' (Office of Review, 1998a). Together these are seen as good indicators of the general occupational health of a school. Although completed by individual members of staff, it is assumed that a school variable is being assessed. A structural model indicating the relationship between the 14 variables is also intended to help decide upon appropriate actions for any particular issue.

The State guidelines recommend that the annual staff survey is carried out about the middle of each school year. The format of the survey includes a number of core areas for all schools but allows individual schools to include

Table 10.2   Fourteen components of effective staff management

1. *School morale*
   Extent of general feeling of energy, enthusiasm and pride among staff

2. *Goal congruence*
   The extent to which there are clear goals to which staff are committed

3. *Supportive leadership*
   The extent to which the leadership are involved in the school and support the work of teachers

4. *Professional interaction*
   Extent of communication and collaboration

5. *Professional development and growth*
   Extent to which teachers are encouraged and given opportunities for professional development

6. *Participative decision-making*
   Extent to which staff are given opportunities to give their views and are asked to participate in decisions

7. *Appraisal and recognition*
   Extent to which staff receive feedback and recognition for their work

8. *Role clarity*
   Extent to which teachers' work objectives inform them of what is expected of them

9. *Curriculum co-ordination*
   Extent to which the curriculum is planned and co-ordinated and involves teachers

10. *Student orientation*
    Extent to which staff encourage students to become responsible and successful

11. *Effective discipline policy*
    Extent to which school agrees and enforces its discipline policy

12. *Student misbehaviour*
    Extent to which student misbehaviour is a problem

13. *Excessive work demands*
    Extent to which staff feel they are overburdened and overworked

14. *School distress*
    Extent to which staff feel anxious, depressed and frustrated.

five questions of their own. Procedures are suggested to ensure that the individual responses are anonymous.

Completing such a survey is valuable since it raises issues and sets an agenda that otherwise might be implicit. For small schools it is suggested that the survey questions could be used as a staff meeting agenda. In any case it is suggested that in addition to forming part of the annual report, the results should be made available for discussion by staff.

Analysis of results

The absolute values of the data do not have any meaning, but various comparisons can aid interpretation of the results:

- comparisons over time
- comparisons with all other schools
- comparisons with 'like' schools
- examining the profile of responses.

In the Victorian context, 'like' schools are those with similar proportions of students who receive government financial assistance (similar to free school meals) and similar proportions of pupils whose first language is not English. While most data can be summarised and compared with benchmarks (CDC) from similar groups of schools, the profile of responses for the staff and parental surveys may also be revealing. In the case of the staff survey, this may indicate diverse views among the staff, relative unanimity or the presence of a small number of disaffected respondents. Guidance has been produced for schools and school councils on the interpretation of the data (Office of Review, 1996f 1998b). Whether the extent of changes from year to year or the differences from benchmarks is sufficient to be noteworthy is left to individual judgement under the guidance of the verifier.

These comparisons are intended to support the interpretation of the results. Trends in the results over time can show improvement or deterioration and the comparison with 'like' schools indicates the relative position of the school compared to its peers. Examination of these trends and comparisons assists an assessment of the significance of the results and inferences about the underlying factors. In this way informed decisions can be made about the need for action.

External verification

The triennial review report is scrutinised by an external independent verifier who is appointed by the verification group which holds the contract for that area. This is followed by a meeting with school representatives to discuss aspects of the review report and their implications for the next school charter. The verifier produces a report following the verification process.

> The verification by an independent reviewer is designed to validate the school's achievements and facilitate agreement between the school and the Department of Education regarding the directions to be incorporated in the next charter.

> The recommendations about the school's goals and priorities agreed at the verification meeting must be incorporated into the school's new charter (Office of Review,1998c, p.6).

The verifier examines the school's self-assessment report and answers three questions:

- Is the school self-assessment supported by the data presented?
- Has anything been overlooked?
- Is there sufficient challenge in the future directions suggested by the school?

The external element of the review process assumes four days of activity for one person – pre-visit, perusal of documentation, a review meeting, presentation of a draft report to the school council and production of a final report. The precise format depends on the reviewer. The review meeting lasts most of one day and may include a tour of the school.

There are recommendations about who should attend the review meeting. These include the president of the school council in addition to senior personnel from the school. The procedures suggest that agreement should be jointly reached with the reviewer about recommendations following the review process. These are contained in a draft verification report which is presented to the school council. The reviewer should also make a presentation to the school staff if asked to do so by the principal.

The final report is signed by the verifier, the principal and the president of the school council and is sent to the Office for Review and to the regional education office. The regional office is expected to support the achievement of individual school charter aims.

The verifier's role is an influential one and the verifier needs to be well-informed both about the Department's plans and priorities and about practices in schools. While there are comparative statistics from other schools for use as a guide to relative performance, the verifier is expected to give guidance on data collection and interpretation. The verifier is also expected to provide feedback to the school on its proposals for the new charter and the extent to which the proposals are sufficiently challenging.

Triennial review

Every three years the annual reports are incorporated into a triennial review of the same issues. The statistics are compared for time trends and are also compared to 'like' schools and to the State average. The statistics for pupil performance are in the form of box plots showing the range and concentration of the data for each student group. At present most pupil performance is teacher assessed although there are some voluntary test results appearing at Years 3, 5, 7 and 9 for comparison.

The report includes data collected by the school and this is collated with observations on the data and proposals for action. This review is circulated to the school council and the external verifier. The task of the external verifier is (a) to approve the process of collecting and collating the data as giving a valid record, and (b) to write a report commenting on the data and suggesting priorities for the next charter. The review and the verifier's report are sent to the Office of Review for the State of Victoria. The latter sends a copy to the appropriate regional office and may follow up any discrepancies between the school's view and the verifier's.

It is generally agreed that schools made too many priorities in their first charter and are being advised to set between two and four in their second charter, depending on school size and complexity of priorities. The expectation is that uncompleted priorities from the first charter will be continued if still considered important and that new ones will be added. The priorities are expected to include State and school priorities.

Three triennial reviews observed

While Brian Fidler was in Melbourne in March 1999, he was permitted to observe three review meetings and study the documentation. This included one primary school and two secondary schools. The review documents produced by the schools were between 60 and 70 pages long, although much of this was computer-produced displays of the analysed data. The verifiers' reports were between 16 and 25 pages. In each case the primary school document was shorter. Different verifiers conducted the three observed review meetings.

The three schools were among the last group to enter the Accountability Framework and hence were among the last to carry out triennial reviews. In some cases, changes at school level such as a school merger had postponed their entry into the Accountability Framework, while in other cases it was suggested that feelings of some antipathy to these processes had caused the delay.

At a conference for verifiers in January 1999, the Office of Review reported that of the first 250 reviews in the first year, 14 schools were deemed to be causing concern. Of these, 11 improved over the following year and three received further attention. In the second year, 40 schools were deemed to be causing concern. The cause of this increase is not clear and may be due to rising expectations of standards or the performance of the second group of schools which entered the 'Schools of the Future' reforms not being as high as the first group. The latter might be expected if it is assumed that the first group to enter were more confident and higher performing schools (Office of Review, 1999).

Observations

The review meeting in the primary school consisted of a group of six staff and the president of the school council. The large group resulted from the delegation of aspects of the review to groups of staff who each reported on their area. Thus the meeting was highly participative with the principal taking a low-key role.

Participation in the two secondary meetings was much more fluid with the principal and vice-principal and a representative of the school council taking part throughout and between four and six others participating for short periods, or joining only for their personal contribution.

In each case the meeting followed the format of the documentation dealing with areas in turn. These were 'charter' goals – curriculum, environment, management, future priorities. Each area consisted of:

- data and comparisons with other schools
- the results of staff deliberations on the data
- implications for the new charter.

Contributions from the various sources of data are collected together to give rounded evidence on each particular area. For example, a consideration of the school environment involves data on student attendance, parental and staff opinion of the school environment, student accident information and student enrolments. In this way a more comprehensive picture can be built up of each area than if only one source of data was used.

It was clear that groups of staff had studied and engaged with the data in each school. They had generally identified a number of implications of the data and had suggested some improvement measures. Occasionally verifiers asked further questions or commented on the data. Sometimes the comments were about the volume or representativeness of the data and suggestions were made about the number of respondents for surveys and the response rate. For example, in one case the data on student absence showed relatively large figures compared with other schools. This did not equate with the impressions of staff and so registration procedures, which were the source of the data, were to be modified to ensure that the results were valid before further action was taken.

At each stage the verifier summed up the discussion to check agreement on what should become recommendations for the new school charter. In the three school reviews there were no noteworthy disagreements between the internal school reviewers and the verifier.

The verifier had studied the documentation prior to the meeting and had identified aspects of the data or implications which he wished to check with the review group.

A major discussion point in each review was the box plots showing student performance in each subject and year group. These had been assessed by staff in accordance with the Curriculum and Standards Framework but showed quite worrying features. As there were data for three years, the same year group could be followed through. Often this indicated that a wide spread of performance within the year group in one year had changed to a very narrow spread the next year for the same group of children. Similarly, student progression in accordance with the Framework showed inconsistent variation from year to year. In each case this was 'explained' by noting that staff were becoming more familiar with assessment on the CSF and such inconsistencies were likely to disappear in the future. However, an unexplored consequence was whether or not teachers used such assessment information to plan their teaching. The three schools had not taken part in the voluntary student tests and hence had no other data to compare with teacher assessments.

It was clear that there was substantial staff ownership of the data and its consequences. However, one of the ironies of the review documentation is that the process – for example, the number of people involved, ways in which they were involved, the length of time over which the review had been conducted – is not documented. This would have provided a useful indication of involvement which could have been discussed at the review meeting. In one case the principal intended to use the verifier's report as a further measure to increase resolve to tackle some difficult issues and suggested to the external verifier that it would be helpful if the report included certain points.

Implications for schools in England and Wales

The assisted school self-review process in Victoria is embedded in the context of the educational assumptions of its various stakeholders. Therefore it will be necessary to translate that experience into suggestions for what might be helpful here.

Firstly, it should be noted that the triennial review is intended to be closely related to the existing school charter and its revision. Without the focus of charter aims, the review process would be much more diffuse. However, the charter has many similarities with school development plans (SDPs) in English schools. SDPs could be developed in importance and stakeholder involvement to provide such a public focus.

Secondly, the process is taken seriously not only because of the professionalism of the participants but also because there is an implied threat that if the external verifier were to suggest aspects of the school's operation which the school was not willing to tackle, the district office personnel would intervene. A local education authority in England would need to take on such an active role of assessing a school's proposals to ensure that it was acting on the review findings.

Thirdly, unlike OfSTED inspections, the process does not reach classroom level. There is no direct observation of teachers and only in primary schools with a single class year group would the performance of an individual teacher receive attention through the scrutiny of pupil performance data in that year group. In England it is possible that individual pupil performance data on external tests may provide at least some indication of the work of individual teachers.

Fourthly, it has been recognised in Victoria that additional actions are needed for schools which are not seen to be capable of improving. The review procedures are suitable for most schools but not for those which are struggling.

Fifthly, the review process is greatly facilitated by specialist computer software (Gurr, 1999). Stored data, on such issues as student and staff absence and pupil performance, are presented and surveys, such as those of parents and staff, are facilitated with regards to sampling and the analysis of resulting statistics. Although these facilities were not without criticism, the reviews would be much more labour intensive and less well presented without such computer assistance.

Sixthly, an irony of the process is that teaching support staff are almost completely ignored. For English schools survey data from such groups would be required since they have come to play an increasingly important role.

Finally, the involvement of the school council in the process ensures that representatives of the community and parents are informed about the performance of the school and play an explicit part in formulating the school's charter or priorities for the next three years. The yearly reviews provide a mandatory, periodic and public monitoring report on progress on these priorities.

Overall, the evidence points to considerable potential for using comparative data collection as an input into school self-review. By using instruments for data collection with a substantial common core it is possible both to collect data which will be of value to an individual school and also to have results where there is common data from a number of 'like schools'. The collection and scrutiny of these data can give a sense of ownership to the findings and also lead to a selective need for further data. With agreed findings there can be informed discussion about their consequences and action needed.

Instruments such as the staff monitoring survey can indicate the feelings of staff in a way which is not ordinarily available and can act as an early warning that things are going wrong. It can also be used as a monitoring device to see if corrective action is working. Such a use can also be found for the parental survey and there is an increasing need for a systematic annual student survey.

A range of data which extends outcomes beyond examination and test results could also be compiled. Victorian schools already have data on, amongst other things, co-curricular, enrichment and compensatory activities which supplement and extend the formal academic curriculum. Where there are problem issues, student behaviour questionnaires could diagnose a need for action and monitor its implementation.

It should, however, be recognised that data of this kind need sensitive treatment and an informed approach to their limitations. Much data will be indicative rather than definitive and too much should not be read into the raw results. There is a potential for injustice. Initially there may be errors in the results, but as the data prove useful and important their accuracy should improve through the process of feedback.

The role of the verifier here is important. They can guide a school in the interpretation of the data and seek to prevent inferences which go beyond the validity of the indicators. On the other hand, verifiers can raise issues which appear to have been overlooked by internal reviewers or which the school seems reluctance to tackle.

Conclusions

The process of self-review using existing and specially collected data which is then compared with that from 'like' schools has much to commend it for schools whose performance is good or improving. This can give flexibility to an individual school to investigate areas of its operation which are seen as particularly important while also giving a general overview of all schools. Assistance from a verifier to ensure that the findings are valid, that inferences do not go beyond the data, and that findings are not overlooked and appropriate action is to be taken, strengthens the process.

As the review process includes mainly factual data and opinions collected on standardised instruments using approved sampling schemes, the results from each school can be used for accountability purposes to assess changes in school performance year by year and hence the performance of the school system. The public yearly reviews by which each school's data are compared with 'like' schools provides an accountability check on the performance of each individual school.

Assisted school reviews are much more economical than OfSTED school inspections. The cost of external verification in Victoria is about 10 per cent of the cost of an OfSTED inspection contract in England. However, a great deal is expected of school staff in the internal review – collecting and collating data, analysing the data for their significance and assessing the need for action. How far this activity would exceed the time staff spend preparing for school inspections in England and Wales is difficult to say, but it should not be assumed that it would be less. However, this does mean that taking the resources employed by the school and inspectors in the current OfSTED inspection arrangements, there would be significant reductions in cost.

While the Victorian approach could not be imported directly, its features could enhance the prospects for school improvement if they were taken up in England with LEAs collating and summarising the common data and identifying 'like' schools (see Chapter 12). There could also be comparisons across LEAs of 'like' schools if instruments and analyses had similar characteristics.

This approach does appear to engage the attention of teachers and the neutrality of the data seems to prevent the adversarial reaction which inspections and judgements by OfSTED inspectors sometimes engender. If, as seems likely, it encourages an evidence-based approach to teaching and management then it has much to commend it.

NOTE

[1] The recent introduction of 'Beacon Schools' has been to spread good practice although receiving visitors is not one of their functions. The notion follows the example of 'Navigator' schools in Victoria, Australia, which are examplar schools for the integration of IT into learning technology.

11

OfSTED and school self-evaluation

The Office for Standards in Education is a powerful and confident organisation that has achieved a great deal during the period of the first round of school inspections (see Chapter 2). Its system of external inspection cannot be altered in fundamental ways without changing the provisions of the 1992 Education Act, but it has nevertheless evolved and improved year by year in response to criticism and to changes in the curriculum (OfSTED,1997a; 1999d). It is, however, strangely ambivalent about self-evaluation and has resisted suggestions that it should be developed as an integral part of the inspection system. It seems to wish to contain the pressure for its introduction as an aspect of the formal inspection process by encouraging schools to develop self-evaluation using the OfSTED Framework (see *School Evaluation Matters*, OfSTED, 1998a). The hope must be that if its use is confined to that of an 'optional extra' or an 'additional management tool', then the Office for Standards in Education will be judged to have taken limited but sensible steps to encourage schools to judge their own progress. In the Foreword to the guide to OfSTED's training materials, the Minister of Education wrote in support of self-evaluation and welcomed its 'firm foundation in the OfSTED Framework' (DfEE/OfSTED, 1999). As noted in Chapter 1, we have called self-evaluation using the OfSTED Framework 'self-inspection' to distinguish it from systems that allow schools to evaluate themselves in their own terms. The minister added that self-evaluation based on the OfSTED criteria ('self-inspection') 'reinforces the message that school self-evaluation and rigorous external inspection of schools go hand in hand'. In fact, they do not because, as we have already noted, there is no agreed policy or approach that is likely to bring self-evaluation and external inspection together. The reasons for OfSTED's reluctance to embrace 'self-inspection' more wholeheartedly are examined in some detail in this chapter. Some characteristics of each approach are shown in Table 11.1. The main characteristics of self-evaluation are taken from MacBeath's (1999) recent work, while those of 'self-inspection' are further explored in Chapter 12.

Table 11.1 Characteristics of methods of self-evaluation (after MacBeath, 1999) and of 'self-inspection' in schools (see Chapter 12)

Self-evaluation	'Self-inspection'
Means that teachers do not have to rely on an external view (1999, p.1)	Brings the external view into the school
Helps schools to know themselves and tell their own story in their own way (p.2)	Allows schools to see themselves as others see them
Used flexibly by schools. Not prescriptive (p.21)	The content of self-inspection is largely predetermined
Challenge to improve comes primarily from within (p.3)	Can be required to be completed by all schools. Deadlines can be set. Can take account of national and local initiatives
Advocated as a valuable management tool: a supplement to external inspection (p.21)	An intrinsic element of OfSTED inspection: takes over some of the functions of external inspection
May be difficult to replicate. Results might require some explanation	Can be replicated and evaluated. Criteria already familiar
Schools must accommodate another set of criteria (p.78)	Same criteria used
Self-evaluation systems are often time-consuming and cumbersome (p.129)	'Self-inspection' has limited aims and is relatively simple
Accountability and self-improvement are seen as two strands of a single interrelated strategy (p.155)	Inspection's accountability and improvement functions can be separated

Our research has suggested that teachers, like OfSTED, are ambivalent about self-evaluation. The case for the introduction of new and possibly elaborate systems is not self-evident. MacBeath (1999), for example, describes the ten 'clusters' of self-evaluation activity in his 'Framework' for self-evaluation (see Table 11.2) and gives five examples of individual indicators for each cluster. Teachers are encouraged, for example, to monitor attainments by looking at random samples of pupils' work, but unlike OfSTED inspections, judgements might also be made of the schools' effectiveness in recognising achievements and identifying young people who rarely experience success at school. It is continuous activity that ebbs and flows across every term of each school year and depends for its effectiveness on its impact on teachers' thinking. MacBeath's framework includes clusters for 'relationships', 'support for learning', 'support for teaching' and 'home–school relationships'. But where is self-evaluation's place in the system and what is its relationship to external inspection? Is it a desirable strategy for schools that are already well organised and where staff are not too concerned about the workload? A local authority adviser is quoted by Mac-Beath as saying, 'The domination of the OfSTED criteria makes it difficult for schools to accommodate another set of criteria' (1999, p.78). It is an important point that needs to be addressed. Self-evaluation will not be accepted by government as a replacement for external inspection and will not, unless circumstances change, gain wide acceptance by teachers as a desirable *addition* to the armoury of management tools that schools have developed to cope with the demands of our 'audit society'.

Table 11.2 Framework for self-evaluation –
10 clusters (from MacBeath, 1999)

1. School climate
2. Relationships
3. Classroom climate
4. Support for learning
5. Support for teaching
6. Time and resources
7. Organisation and communication
8. Equity
9. Recognition of achievement
10. Home-school links.

Can schools evaluate themselves?

OfSTED is unlikely to work against its own self-interest and, as MacBeath suggests, make itself 'as redundant as possible' (p.1) by allowing systems of self-evaluation largely to replace its current functions. In his recent annual report, the chief inspector argued: 'Too many headteachers do not really know what is happening in the classrooms of their schools' (OfSTED, 1999b). HMCI went on to suggest that heads' lack of knowledge can be explained by their inattention to the systematic evaluation of both the quality of teaching and the standards achieved by pupils. Without this, he suggests, 'development planning is clearly impossible and target setting little more than pious aspiration' (OfSTED, 1999b, p.18).

There is evidence to support HMCI's point of view because OfSTED's own study of 100 primary and secondary schools is reported to have found that schools had a reasonably accurate view of their strengths but much less insight into their weaknesses. The study (which has not been published) is cited in *School Evaluation Matters* (OfSTED, 1998a) to support the argument that the impressions that heads gain in the absence of systematic monitoring are frequently wrong. It discovered that two-thirds of the key issues in secondary school inspection reports and almost three-quarters of those in primary school reports were not identified as priorities before the inspection began. However, as our own research has shown, most heads believe that they are fully aware of their school's strengths and weaknesses and frequently commented that inspectors cannot tell them anything they do not already know. They took the common-sense viewpoint that 'a good head' ought to be aware of the school's strengths and weaknesses and some concluded that inspection was therefore an 'expensive waste of time'. Headteachers' motives for adopting this stance are not difficult to understand. To believe otherwise would be an admission that they were unaware of shortcomings which the inspection team was able to identify as a result of its brief visit to the school.

In Chapter 5 we described our study, in which heads were asked to predict the key issues that they expected to see in their schools' inspection reports, which reinforces the findings of the OfSTED research. Although the heads' predictions were rarely confirmed by the inspectors' judgements, most heads believed their inspection report was accurate and that their key issues raised important matters for the school's attention. One possible interpretation of this study and of OfSTED's own research is, as HMCI has claimed, that heads really do not know what is going on in their own schools. This casts doubt on the wisdom of developing systems for self-evaluation and provides a convincing reason for not taking their results too seriously. However, viewed from the schools' perspective, we might equally ask why matters that concern heads before the inspection (and are predicted to become important key issues) are not picked up and given high priority by the inspectors. It is possible that the dialogue that takes place in the inspection week convinces heads of the importance of OfSTED's rather than their own findings. This would be a serious concern because it would be a further illustration of the way that inspection has 'colonised' thinking and undermined heads' and teachers' confidence in their judgements of their own schools. It may be that every possible weakness occurs to heads in the anxiety-ridden months before an inspection. This could explain why they feel their inspection report was unsurprising. However, it is important to ask why inspectors are not more influenced by the school's own analyses of its strengths and shortcomings. Do inspectors learn about the matters that concerned the staff before the inspection began? Does the RgI feel inadequate if the report merely identifies areas for development that were already listed in the school's development or improvement plan? Is it inspectors' role to tell heads and governors about their school and hopefully surprise them with most of their findings?

It is not obvious that external inspection provides a better basis for school improvement than teachers' professional judgements. The latter may have been formed as the result of a great deal of observation and a large number of discussions with colleagues, pupils, parents and governors. The fact that these judgements do not arise from bureaucratic processes is not sufficient reason to assume they are unsystematic, but this is usually an untested assumption whenever assertions about the importance of external inspection are made. Russell (1996) briefly reviews the research evidence and concludes that 'it is hard to find a strong research basis for the belief that effective leadership and effective schools depend on specific formal processes of individual and institutional review' (p.327).

Russell goes on to explain that staff, who are continually keeping matters under review through reflection and professional discussion, may be adopting a superior approach to the one advocated by OfSTED. However, as schools are subjected to external inspection, they are likely to adopt 'internal bureaucratic processes' of their own and this may not be in their best interests. It is important to add, nevertheless, that external inspection and the formal recording of judgements are essential for purposes of public accountability and that self-evaluation, however effectively carried out, would not be an acceptable alternative.

Some of the schools in our case studies that received very good reports felt that inspectors needed to find something to say. Their headteachers had not been able to predict the outcomes of their inspection and had given the key issues a low priority. OfSTED inspections tend to be 'done to' rather than 'done for' schools and it may be that inspectors' desire to maintain a proper 'distance' prevents them from taking more of a lead from school staff and governors. Inspectors, however, have the advantage of having worked in a large number of schools, of making systematic observations and of using a variety of evidence with which to make judgements. They are also able to compare notes with colleagues who have collected much the same evidence using the same criteria but their observations are made over a brief time span (a snapshot) when the school is not working normally.

Schools have access to much more evidence about all of the aspects covered by the Inspection Framework, but it is rarely collected systematically or analysed with the same degree of care or detachment. However, to present inspection as an 'objective' process carried out by 'experts' tends to suggest that its value is confined to its outcomes. Involvement in the process is valuable in its own right because the insights gathered along the way may provide teachers with a better understanding of the aspects of their work in school that would benefit from further development.

It is all too easy to fall into the trap of assuming that 'inspectors know best', but equally it cannot be assumed that school self-evaluation can make a significant contribution to school development if it relies on the assumption that 'teachers know best'. The situation in which heads and inspectors find themselves leads each group to justify their role. Inspectors have reasons to take an independent line, which is not much influenced by the school's view, in order to demonstrate the usefulness of the inspection. Heads have reasons to view the inspectors' findings as 'telling us what we already know' and asserting that matters were 'already under review'. There is, therefore, an unhelpful tension at the heart of inspection which contributes to making the process unnecessarily 'distant'. Continuous evaluation informed from a variety of perspectives and removed from the threat of 'naming and shaming' need not lay claims to 'objectivity' and need not be conducted in a public arena in order to stimulate improvements or draw attention to teachers whose teaching would benefit from support and additional in-service training. It must, however, be done systematically and be capable of making judgements about the standards achieved by pupils and the quality of education which is provided.

Is there room for self-evaluation?

In *School Evaluation Matters* (OfSTED, 1998a) teachers are told that 'Inspectors ask the same questions about the school as you do.' Tactfully the authors omit HMCI's rider 'but arrive at quite different answers' and prefer, instead, to explain how the Inspection Framework can be reinterpreted as 'a practical template' for school self-evaluation. Despite this, the reinspection process simply requires inspectors to report on progress since the last inspection and thus, arguably, misses an opportunity to involve schools in presenting their own evidence. The fact that schools are gathering useful information for self-evaluation purposes is, no doubt, recognised as a strength by inspectors. From January 2000, heads are expected to produce a written account of the outcomes of self-evaluation as part of their pre-inspection report but this is not the same as finding a place *within* the Inspection Framework for the content of self-evaluation to influence the outcomes of the report. The Framework for the reinspection of schools addresses this in a very limited way by including schools' capacity for change as one of the criteria for inspectors to consider (OfSTED, 1998c).

Thus far, we have noted that inspection teams do not involve the head or school governors for even a short time in the inspection except as a source of information when they are interviewed by members of the inspection team. The inspection is not seen as an opportunity for schools to gain first-hand experience of the process by contributing directly to the interpretation of the evidence on which judgements about the school are made. There are no requirements for schools to collect data for use in the inspection, although they can certainly expect to be criticised if there are few signs that they have monitored standards, teaching quality, the curriculum and progress in improving the school. There is little sense, officially, of a partnership in school improvement which might not only provide better inspection data but could also give teachers and inspectors new insights into the school's strengths and weaknesses. Heads' apparent lack of knowledge of their own schools and the areas for development is not only seen as the justification for OfSTED inspection but as a serious problem which needs to be separately addressed. The obvious solution of changing the OfSTED approach and involving heads, governors and staff in the inspection process is not a suggestion that has been welcomed. If this is, as we believe, an accurate summary of OfSTED's current position, we need to ask about its implications for the future of self-evaluation and for the inspection system.

OfSTED's public stance is to promote self-evaluation (self-inspection) through persuasion and the provision of accredited trainers, guidance and materials. It appears to want to treat the subject positively as long as it is just a supplement to the serious business of external inspection. Much is made of the point that school self-evaluation can never be a substitute for rigorous and periodic independent inspection. The DfEE/OfSTED guidance leaflet to schools on self-evaluation explains that external inspection is 'essential if schools are to be held accountable for the public funds they receive, and to provide an objective, external and expert view of their performance' (DfEE/OfSTED, 1999).

John MacBeath, a well-known champion of the cause of self-evaluation in schools, and whose work we have already referred to, described a meeting with HMCI to discuss self-evaluation. He notes:

> Discussions were civilised and robust but the Chief Inspector saw self-evaluation as something that had been tried and had failed and the door was closed after us, politely but firmly (1999, p.71).

HMCI might well have had in mind the attempts during the 1980s to create ready-made systems for self-evaluation. For example, the *Guidelines for Review and Internal Development in Schools (GRIDS)* (see McMahon *et al.*, 1984) was a complex, five-stage, process-oriented, evaluation system which was elaborate and time-consuming and fell into disuse before it could have any great effect on schools. Earley and Fletcher-Campbell (1992) point out that it was essentially 'democratic in principle'. It involved, for example, a phase in which the staff of the school were widely consulted to ascertain their priorities for development. Evidence was then collected to determine the perceived effectiveness of existing policy and practice. There were no arrangements for classroom monitoring and, because of the prevailing climate of opinion, it might have been very difficult for any head or head of department to assert his or her right to monitor teaching quality by making observations of teachers during lessons. Approaches to quality, such as Total Quality Management (TQM) which seeks to make all employees think constantly about how the functions which they perform might be improved, have been described as 'mechanistic' and the self-evaluation system which currently operates in the Further Education (FE) sector, described by Melia (1995) and Dixon (1996), has been too easily criticised for its lack of a sharp critical edge (Kelly, 1996). Doubts about the adequacy of self-assessment in FE colleges are reinforced by a recent Further Education Funding Council report on self-assessment (Bainbridge, 1999) which concluded that more than 30 per cent of curriculum grades awarded by inspectors were one or two grades lower than those the colleges had given to themselves.

Whatever the reasons for the chief inspector's failure to endorse self-evaluation, it is not difficult to understand why there might be some reluctance within government to embrace it wholeheartedly. OfSTED would be concerned that inspectors' impartiality would be threatened if the 'distance' between inspectors and teachers were to be removed. There would be a suspicion that many heads and teachers would want to be involved in the inspection process so that they could provide information to defend the school from criticism. There might be a concern about confidentiality if teachers were too closely involved in discussions about their school and the performance of staff. Perhaps the most important worry is that the inspectors themselves would be inhibited in carrying out their duties if they became too closely involved with teachers. It is not, as the DfEE/OfSTED guidance maintains, self-evident that the inspectors are more expert than those whom they inspect or that their judgements are 'objective' and reliable (DfEE/OfSTED, 1999). However, there may be a concern that the inspection system would be undermined if teachers were placed in a strong position to make successful challenges to the evidence on which judgements were based. Some RgIs reported their concerns about team inspectors who seemed to be reluctant to take 'hard decisions' about poor quality teaching, inadequate leadership and low expectations. There may be a fear, therefore, that closer working relationships between inspectors and teachers would make it even more difficult for inspection teams to make clear decisions about failing schools and poorly performing teachers.

Whatever the inspectors themselves may believe, they are not there to be helpful. They are paid to report on standards and on the strengths and weaknesses of schools. The notion of a genuine role for self-evaluation may seem to OfSTED and many inspectors to introduce data of unknown worth and risk the 'contamination' of the judgement process and a loss of independence and 'objectivity'. There may also be doubts about whether schools, after some initial enthusiasm, would be capable of sustaining such demanding and time-consuming activity. It is a perspective that RgIs who want to provide support and advice (see Chapter 8) and headteachers who believe that OfSTED inspection is 'free consultancy' should keep in view. The case against self-evaluation seems to contain some convincing arguments, but we do not yet know whether the ideas of MacBeath and others would receive wide support in English schools.

As we have shown in the previous chapter, an alternative approach to these issues in Victoria, Australia, was to recognise that school self-evaluation or review could be a worthwhile activity for schools. It can produce results of value to the individual school and also for the evaluation of national priorities in education, but an external component is needed to ensure that the process is sufficiently rigorous. Thus to meet both accountability and developmental purposes, the school review process uses a number of standard instruments to gather data on a range of performance indicators. It also employs an external verifier to ensure that there is a consistency of approach in all schools, that interpretations of the data are appropriate and that evaluation leads to relevant action. This approach directs attention to outcomes in the form of student performance data but not, as in OfSTED's case, to the process of teaching. In view of the difficulty of validly judging teaching performance, the high cost of attempting to do so and the difficulties of connecting teaching performance with student outcomes, the Victorian approach probably provides better value for money.

Schools' commitment to monitoring and evaluation

One further issue seems relevant. Why, if the benefits are so important, should decisions about self-evaluation affect the OfSTED inspection process? No doubt there are many schools that coped well with inspection and can demonstrate an impressive record of action taken on the basis of their own systematically gathered evaluation data. However, as Chapter 8 noted, when RgIs were asked to recommend changes to the inspection system, they wanted to find a role for self-evaluation, but primary school heads did not show the same enthusiasm. Heads of primary schools were fully aware of the emphasis that OfSTED places on monitoring and evaluation, but some found it difficult to find the time or the staff to monitor teaching quality and some preferred to consider other priorities.

The case studies demonstrated that monitoring was often difficult to organise and heads' good intentions were all too frequently unfulfilled. Monitoring the curriculum to ensure that it was broad, balanced and provided adequate coverage for all aspects of the National Curriculum was perceived to be an onerous task. Monitoring progress through the written work of pupils and records of progress on individual targets was also very time-consuming. The regular monitoring of the quality of teaching in every classroom in the school could be difficult to arrange. It often meant obtaining the services of a supply teacher to provide the curriculum co-ordinators with opportunities to observe their subject specialism being taught to every year group. Some heads and co-ordinators, particularly in small primary schools, believed that inspectors' requirements did not take sufficient account of the practical difficulties or the more urgent demands that must inevitably be given priority.

> The problem is lack of non-contact time. Resources are not available to release teachers to monitor in classrooms. What's the point of monitoring when literacy hour is coming in and we have staff who have no idea what it means (English co-ordinator inner-city school).

> I am a teaching head and I worry that I have not found time for monitoring (head of a rural school).

When asked about monitoring, one urban school head's reaction was tinged with more than a hint of desperation. It was the strongest expression of a fairly common response of heads who felt too hard pressed to monitor. It was a reminder of Fullan's (1991) warning about the effects of handing down new tasks to teachers who may already be struggling to cope with the considerable demands of the daily round in school.

You have to cut your coat according to your cloth. I have problems with an NQT who has just resigned. I am teaching. I am keeping a million balls in the air. The monitoring will have to wait. I tried to see one teacher but she was absent on the day. I have only done one monitoring this half term because I cannot do any more. I am not saying it's best but I am doing what I can. I work like a Trojan until midnight and I am just standing still.

It was an understandable response but not one that gives monitoring the priority that OfSTED believes it should have. Heads were generally aware of the significance that OfSTED attached to monitoring but did not seem to be able to give it sufficient priority to satisfy the inspectors' requirements. Some schools, it seems, would not have volunteered and had required an inspection to persuade them to monitor their activities.

Conclusion

Few commentators, if any, would want to suggest that OfSTED inspections should be replaced entirely by systems of school self-evaluation. OfSTED's current plans are to provide schools with appropriate guidance and materials and invite them to evaluate their activities regularly using the OfSTED criteria. However, there can be no certainty that schools will consider this a priority or be able to find the time or resources to conduct self-evaluation (self-inspection) rigorously and systematically.

There is a continuing suspicion that self-evaluation is a 'soft option' and that schools will simply take the opportunity to present themselves in the most favourable light. It follows that only an external inspection that maintains a proper distance and neutrality can be depended upon to provide an independent and unbiased opinion. It appears that OfSTED's preoccupation with its accountability function prevents inspectors from giving attention to school improvement. It is why the final chapter makes recommendations about 'self-inspecting' rather than 'self-evaluating' schools and recommends that provision for the improvement and accountability functions of inspection should be separated.

Action planning on the basis of the outcomes of an OfSTED inspection assumes a deficit model of performance that reduces the process of school improvement to a perpetual attempt to eradicate weaknesses. Inspection results should be only *one* element in a continuous and hopefully more creative process of school improvement. The final chapter makes some suggestions about the modifications to the Inspection Framework which, we believe, would help to separate inspection's accountability and school improvement functions, combat its ill-effects on staff and pupils and allow schools to seek greater autonomy.

12

The self-inspecting school and the future of inspection

Why change is desirable

The research evidence seems to support the view that OfSTED inspections, despite the impressive achievements described in Chapter 2, have a number of significant limitations which, we have argued, ought to be given further consideration. Besides being expensive and time-consuming, inspections disrupt schools for considerable periods of time and distract teachers from the essential business of teaching their pupils. They create high levels of stress in teaching staff, inhibit improvement both before and after inspection and make it more difficult for heads and senior managers to manage their schools effectively. Six of these significant imperfections of the current system of inspection have been chosen to illustrate the argument. These are listed in Table 12.1.

Table 12.1 Inspection's imperfections – six examples

---

1. Inspection is not an effective catalyst for school improvement in the pre-inspection period

2. Inspection is not an effective catalyst for school improvement in the immediate post-inspection period

3. The apprehension that inspection creates in schools causes many heads, teachers and governors to react inappropriately

4. The feedback given to teachers rarely has much effect on their classroom practice

5. Inspection does not do enough to foster the growth of skills in self-evaluation

6. Judgements may be unreliable and yet have serious consequences for individuals

---

Preparation for inspection or opportunity for development?

Inspection is not an effective catalyst for school improvement in the pre-inspection period. There is a widespread reluctance among heads to see the pre-inspection period as a spur to action and an opportunity to inject a sense of urgency into improvements which are being pursued through the school development plan (see Chapter 3). Teachers are anxious and overburdened in the months before an inspection is due and it was often necessary to put planned developments 'on hold'. Lengthy periods of notice were given to schools of an impending inspection in the belief that they would seize the opportunity to develop and improve in the period of a year or more before the inspectors arrived. However, a gradual reduction in the length of the notification period has taken place and is a tacit recognition that the pre-inspection period has not proved as effective a catalyst for school improvement as had been envisaged. The Parliamentary Select Committee on OfSTED inspections (see Chapter 8) suggested a further reduction in the pre-inspection period to only four weeks. Schools, however, anticipate inspections long before the formal announcement is made and the emphasis on preparation for inspection, rather than school development, reduces the opportunities for the achievement of 'improvement through inspection'. Much of the effort of teachers in the pre-inspection period gains diminishing returns which are, arguably, of only marginal relevance to any of the judgements that inspectors are likely to make (see Chapter 3).

Exhaustion and anti-climax or renewed enthusiasm?

Inspection is not an effective catalyst for school improvement in the immediate post-inspection period. School improvements were often adversely affected in the aftermath of an inspection to allow staff time to recover. The recovery time was commonly six months or two school terms, but some heads reported that staff experienced the 'post-inspection blues' for a year or more. The stress and exhaustion which commonly occurs in the period after inspection has become a recognisable post-inspection phenomenon. This not only has adverse effects on school development but, in some cases, causes lasting distress to teachers, including some who emerge from the inspection process with credit.

The Parliamentary Select Committee heard a great deal about inspection's side-effects but concluded: 'schools will become more used to the fact of inspection and may thus see it as less of a traumatic experience' (House of Commons, 1999a, paragraph 35). In our view it is not an answer that can be relied upon because it seems to imply that schools act like individuals who, having been 'traumatised' once, can steady themselves when the same event occurs a second time. Reinspections will often be reporting on shifting populations of heads, staff, children and governors who happen to have congregated at the same site some six years or so after the school was first inspected. We do not know how the 'school' will react and cannot predict how those teachers who have remained substantially in the same role within a school will anticipate a reinspection.

Apprehension or confidence?

The apprehension that inspection creates in schools causes many heads, teachers and governors to react inappropriately. Headteachers may have more substantial experience of schools than some members of their inspection team. However, their characteristic response during an inspection is often an anxious desire to please rather than a response that signals that the relationship is not one of subservience in the face of authority. Those who allow, if not encourage, inspectors to play the role of the school's 'temporary overseer' during their time in school are not playing a fully professional role. Given the rules of the inspection game, their response is understandable and it may help the school if some degree of deference meets their inspection team's expectations (see Chapter 4).

Despite RgIs' strong desire to present themselves as friendly and helpful and their success in convincing heads that they are 'sensitive' and 'professional', it is far from clear that support and advice forms a vital part of their role. There are significant contradictions between inspectors' aspirations, teachers' beliefs and the development of an inspection system that was, arguably, not developed to provide support for schools.

Explanation of gradings or suggestions for development?

The feedback given to teachers rarely has much effect on their classroom practice. They have welcomed the addition of feedback sessions as a routine part of the inspection process but they want to know how the inspectors have assessed the quality of their teaching. However, it was sometimes difficult to find adequate time for these feedback sessions and inspectors were unable to prepare for them as thoroughly as they had hoped. Our case studies revealed that teachers had not normally been told anything which caused them to alter their practice and none could recall being given any substantial help or valuable advice. Almost one-half of the RgI sample had at least some concerns about the teacher feedback system.

Passive recipient or active skill development?

Inspection does not do enough to foster the growth of skills in self-evaluation. There are doubts about the feasibility of self-evaluation in schools and an official suspicion that the process may lack the rigour of external inspection. Heads, it might be suggested, would be tempted to concentrate on comfortable targets with only marginal relevance to standards and the quality of education and, in these circumstances, self-evaluation would have little or no impact.

Trusted judgement or cause for concern?

Judgements may be unreliable and yet have serious consequences for individuals. Several commentators have been critical of the reliability of inspectors' judgements of teaching quality. For example, Millett and Johnson (1998b), discussing the reliability of judgements of primary school mathematics, comment that inspectors are likely to 'share a disparity' in their beliefs about mathematics teaching which 'may well be coloured by their own experiences' and should be investigated. Fitz-Gibbon (1997) has noted that disagreements between would-be inspectors in training sessions are not unusual. One of our authors (NF) also noted, during a one-day literacy hour training session attended by experienced inspectors, that wide discrepancies were common when the course members were asked to make judgements of video recordings of lessons. In another training course it seemed that experienced teachers and heads undertaking initial inspector training were consistently giving higher grades than the 'official judgement' allowed. A study conducted by OfSTED (Matthews *et al.*, 1998) gives a rather different impression. It compared 173 sets of paired lesson observations in classrooms and discovered that there was agreement in 66 per cent of cases and that 97 per cent of judgements were within one grade of each other. The study was carried out using volunteer inspectors and, as Fidler *et al.* (1998) have noted, 'a volunteer sample is likely to be highly biased by including more confident and experienced observers.' It is concluded that 66 per cent agreement may indicate the highest level of agreement which can be expected between inspectors. RgIs, however, are concerned with judgements of team inspectors which they believe are not consistent with the evidence, but the main complaint is about team inspectors who fail to make 'clear', 'sharp' or 'precise' statements. Like poor writing, this lack of decisiveness (or awareness of complexity) leaves the lead inspector with difficulties which must be resolved before the report can be issued. Registered inspectors' comments complain of 'blandness', of a 'lack of clarity' and of inspectors who 'spend too much time on description and too little on judgement'. Lead inspectors, it appears, are intolerant of ambiguity and in favour of statements which leave no room for uncertainty about any of the judgements being made.

These disagreements about the accuracy of inspectors' judgements and the effectiveness of their reports are a useful reminder that in any debate about inspection and 'self-inspection', we are not dealing with perfect processes but with imperfect judgements made by fallible human beings working under pressure in often difficult circumstances. As the chief inspector himself has recognised, 'inspection is not and cannot be objective in a scientific way. It is, as I have said . . . best described as an act of disciplined subjectivity' (*Guardian*, 5 October 1999). It is a reminder too that alternatives to the current system of inspection will also have their weaknesses and are likely to suffer from inaccuracies and inconsistencies of judgement. Any revisions to the Inspection Framework should, among other things, aim to increase the number of observations on which judgements are made and thus increase their reliability. In our view, schools involved in continuous self-inspection would be able to make more reliable judgements.

Whose interests are served by external inspection?

Any discussion of the future development of OfSTED inspection should consider seriously whether its twin purposes of school improvement and public accountability are compatible and recognise that the relationships between the two is problematic. We have argued that there can be no genuine partnership between schools and inspectors while the balance of power is so uneven and the penalties for failing the inspection involve such high stakes. Why would any head with the school's best interests at heart willingly take part in a process which might disrupt pupils' education, upset the staff, anger the parents and destroy the headteacher's own credibility? Why would they help the inspection team to uncover weaknesses which could have a deleterious effect on the school's reputation? It ought not to be the naïve and new headteachers who talk openly to their inspector colleagues. Patients do not visit their doctor and refuse to mention their symptoms. A motorist would be unlikely to call out a mechanic and pretend that the car is in perfect working order and it would be unusual to hire a cleaner and then hide the dust.

However, there are conditions, with distinct parallels in the OfSTED inspection process, when these apparently irrational behaviours would occur. For example, if the doctor was conducting the examination to see if the individual is medically fit to remain in employment, most people who hoped to keep their job would be unlikely to do or say anything that might adversely affect their chances of being given a clean bill of health. Similarly, if the mechanic is from the Automobile Association and acting on behalf of a potential buyer, the car's owner may not be quite as forthcoming as with the mechanic at the local garage. If the cleaners are likely to tell your friends about your unhygienic living conditions, you might well feel too embarrassed to let them see the rooms that are in most need of attention. In the same way, heads must ask themselves in whose interests the inspectors are acting and, in the light of this decision, come to a conclusion about their general stance and tactics. It is the moment when they have to make a judgement about whether OfSTED is acting for or against their interests. The point is not lost on headteachers. One primary head, who was himself an RgI, remarked, 'I left it to them', and another experienced headteacher commented rather bitterly that, 'If inspections cost £35,000 they need no help from me.' In fact the average primary school inspection costs much less than this, but if the costs to the school are included in the total, the figure which the head quoted would be realistic. A lower figure would, in any case, do little to reassure headteachers who decided to 'give nothing away'.

The crucial issue is not one of self-development versus external judgement because the doctor, the mechanic and the cleaner are all 'external'.

However, our reaction to them and our response to their judgements is determined, in part, by our perception of whose interests they are serving. Hargreaves (1995), amongst others, believes that the most effective audit of a school comes about by 'neither internal self-evaluation nor external inspection' and advocates 'a combination of both' (p.120). However, it would be necessary to ensure that a mixture of approaches did not simply combine the 'games playing', which external inspection encourages, with the self-delusion and imprecision to which school self-evaluation can be prone (Earley, 1998b). There is an added danger that inspectors could be seen as assembling information for the prosecution and that the purpose of self-evaluation would be to collect evidence with the intention of contradicting the inspection findings. This would not only threaten inspectors' objectivity and detachment but might even make improvement through inspection more difficult to attain. It seems safe to assume that any function inspection might have in serving the needs of schools or supporting their efforts to develop and improve is not a high priority. OfSTED inspection, we must conclude, was not created and has not been developed with this intention.

It is also difficult to sustain the argument that a function of external inspection is to provide information about schools to inform consumer choice and allow parents and prospective parents to find the best school for their child. There are some parents, particularly in large towns and cities, who have become adept at making arrangements for their children to attend the school of their choice. When schools are oversubscribed, this might mean special pleading, complex travel arrangements or even, in some cases, moving house if this can guarantee a place in a sought-after school. There is little evidence, however, that OfSTED inspection reports have had a major influence on parents who are keenly interested in the quality of their children's education. Schools with 'serious weaknesses' and those identified to be in need of 'special measures' should expect recruitment of new students and staff to be more difficult than usual, but they would be unlikely to experience a mass exodus of existing pupils. Many parents may feel that, in their particular location or circumstances, there is no choice and factors like length and cost of the child's journey and the need to maintain contact with school friends from the same locality are likely to be the major considerations when selecting schools. It seems reasonable to conclude that informing consumer choice, although ideologically important, cannot have been a vital reason for the creation of OfSTED.

The inescapable and in some ways rather obvious conclusion is that the prime purpose of OfSTED inspection is to make schools accountable to government and, by proxy, to the taxpayer and the nation at large. In this view it is important not only to be assured that most schools are meeting national expectations and represent 'value for money' but also to create a mechanism for exposing those that are judged to be unsatisfactory. Inspection is, therefore, a mechanism for ensuring that schools are made aware of their responsibilities to seek improvements and play their part in raising national standards. The first round of inspection was successful in achieving this aim and reinspection, it might be argued, now has the rather limited intention of providing a warning to schools that need a further reminder of their obligations.

The introduction of a shortened or 'light touch' inspection for 'good' schools suggests that there is some official recognition that the first round of inspection has changed the context of future inspections. It is now difficult to sustain an argument that the future of inspection must mean that 'more of the same' is required. The arrangements for differentiated inspections sensibly acknowledge that, for accountability purposes, not all schools require a full inspection. However, if inspectors were charged only with a responsibility to help schools to improve, most schools would reject 'light touch' as a less than thorough job. Like businesses which had hired management consultants, schools would want to receive the most comprehensive report that could be afforded and target the attention of their consultants where it was considered they could be of most value.

Accountability and school improvement?

Would it be possible for OfSTED teams to work more effectively for school improvement without sacrificing anything which is fundamental to their accountability role? The most likely answer is that it would not and that some sacrifices would have to be made. If OfSTED inspection teams were to present themselves as experts who provided management information that could be used to improve standards and the quality of education which the school provided, the nature of inspection would be changed. Inspectors whose instant reaction is 'this is precisely what we are doing!' are failing to appreciate that OfSTED inspection teams are not always perceived in this way and may be seen in the role of judge and jury rather than that of helpful consultants. Furthermore, the sacrifices needed to change these perceptions might be difficult or unacceptable in the current climate. Public accountability is served by openness, the publication of reports, summaries to parents, press reports and the exposure of weak and failing schools. The process is supported by the clear and honest identification of weaknesses in management and teaching and unacceptably low educational standards. To do otherwise would make the inspection system vulnerable to charges of covering up matters which parents and the general public have the right to know or of issuing bland reports which would simply shelter and perpetuate poor teaching and low standards of attainment. It is unlikely that any of this would be readily given up by a society which is aware of the cost of poor quality education and its implications for future generations of children. Radical solutions that might mean replacing external inspection with self-evaluation methods or importing quality assurance and quality development systems from outside education (e.g. Investors in People, the

Business Excellence Model) would be unlikely to be well received. However, the difficulty with the present system of OfSTED inspection is that it is not generally perceived by headteachers to be an approach which has school improvement high enough on its agenda and this, we believe, is *the* issue which ought to be addressed.

The relationship of consultants to schools would be very different. It would be clear that their responsibility would be to the client which they serve. They would be expected to work with school staff to bring about improvements, use their expertise to give advice and suggest changes for which they would feel responsible to the head, senior managers and the governing body. Where serious weaknesses were found they would report them to the head and governors but not to the press and public. Consultants and advisers would expect to see the school working normally and not for a few prearranged days into which staff had invested weeks and sometimes months of careful preparation. In fact, we might predict that governing bodies and heads, whether new or experienced, would welcome such service and, in this climate, schools would be more willing to provide 'warts and all' evidence of their own and apply a rigour to 'self-inspection' which might otherwise be missing. This, however, presupposes a set of national expectations, working assumptions and relationships that are quite different from those reflected in the perceptions of heads during the first round of inspections.

In our view, OfSTED should continue to look critically at the claim that inspections are concerned with school improvement: particularly in those schools not found to be weak or failing. There is a possibility that OfSTED's claim to be achieving 'improvement through inspection' prevents sufficient attention being given to the school improvement process. We need to ask how schools can take charge of the process and yet be supported in their efforts to improve. If schools did accept responsibility for at least part of their own inspection, they might need to be assured that it was not simply a new set of administrative tasks for them to deal with or an 'optional extra' that had no discernible effects in lessening the burden of external inspection. Schools need to be persuaded that the time and nervous energy that we have argued is squandered and misdirected before, during and after an OfSTED inspection can be put to better use. Could LEAs working together with OfSTED help to restore confidence and support school development? Should inspection, unambiguously aimed at making the school accountable, follow a school improvement phase with critical comments from OfSTED inspectors being confined to those schools that had not made satisfactory progress?

The reactions of heads and staff to inspections should not be ignored. The Parliamentary Select Committee on the work of OfSTED may have recognised the pressure that inspection inflicts on schools, but it seemed to suggest that teachers had often overreacted and had become unnecessarily anxious. It decided that the 'key challenge is to change the way in which some schools view inspection, so that they see it as a useful tool, not an external threat' (House of Commons, 1999a, paragraph 35). The Select Committee did not, however, suggest any fundamental revisions to the Inspection Framework that would build confidence, emphasise development or help schools to feel some sense of shared ownership of the inspection process.

An approach to the development of 'self-inspecting' schools is needed which will touch every school in the country and not just those with a ready-made enthusiasm for self-evaluation and improvement. In our view, this means incorporating 'self-inspection' into the OfSTED process, which currently comments on the effectiveness of school self-evaluation but does not take sufficient account of its findings. It is not enough simply to convince schools of the benefits of conducting their own systematic monitoring and evaluation. For many, it will also be necessary to demonstrate that their efforts are acknowledged and that there is a trade-off between OfSTED inspection and 'self-inspection'. It may also be important to emphasise 'a school improvement phase' of the inspection process which would provide the separation of OfSTED's accountability and improvement functions. This, we believe, would represent a significant step forward and one that could be taken without adding to the current workload of schools.

It is important to ask whether we want inspection to remain for all time as a process that is motivated by a desire for greater centralised control and the belief that higher standards can best be obtained by exerting pressure for improvement and punishing those who fail to perform satisfactorily. The strategy has certainly had an effect and teachers now generally support the belief that they should be made publicly accountable for the standards of their pupils' attainments and the quality of education that they provide. It may be time to move on and give more emphasis to the 'support side' of the pressure/support continuum.

The 'self-inspection' schedule

In Victoria, Australia (see Chapter 10), the schools' annual survey allows them to combine questions of their own with those of the State Education Department, and in Chapter 8, we noted that heads would like the opportunity to select some of the foci for inspection. A 'self-inspecting' school should have its own vigorous programme of monitoring and evaluation but, in addition, should monitor aspects of its work using the criteria from the Inspection Framework. 'Self-inspection' is a continuous process which, in an obvious way, would *increase* OfSTED's influence on schools, but in another very important respect would reduce it by breaking the cycle of overreaction, panic, exhaustion and anticlimax that has become characteristic of many conventional inspections. What is inspected can, in part, be prescribed to meet the need for the monitoring of national targets and there should be some insistence that schools keep pupil progress and teaching quality at the heart of their annual self-inspection process. For example, 'self-inspecting' schools could devise annually a schedule for self-inspection that recognised the school's obligation to monitor nationally agreed targets and make provision to assess progress and teaching quality against the OfSTED Framework criteria. The schedule would include other areas for self-evaluation that would support the school's own priorities to be addressed through its normal planning processes. Figures 12.1 and 12.2 describe in broad outline a suggested revision of the current system of inspection that would return a major part of OfSTED's school improvement function to the schools and overcome many of the shortcomings summarised in Table 12.1. This separation of school improvement activity would provide all heads, teachers and governors with opportunities to gain valuable insights into the strengths and weaknesses of their own school and to target their in-service education and staff development activities more accurately.

How, then, might the proposed system work? Pupils' progress would need to be monitored constantly and there would need to be a requirement for teachers to collate and analyse assessment data for each pupil and discuss its implications for lesson and curriculum planning and the allocation of resources. Most schools review pupils' attendance and behaviour regularly, but those with difficulties in these areas might need to give them a high priority in their self-inspection schedule over a period of years. Again it would not be difficult to provide guidance about the monitoring of attendance and behaviour which helped schools to decide how much effort should be devoted to this activity. Some activities like the monitoring of standards should be conducted in conjunction with the LEA, which would be required to provide comparative data and to discuss the school's self-inspection data with staff and governors during each school year. Many LEAs are doing this already but the process does not have a formal place within the inspection system.

Self-inspection would thus become the constant application of a systematic programme of monitoring, evaluating and planning which applied

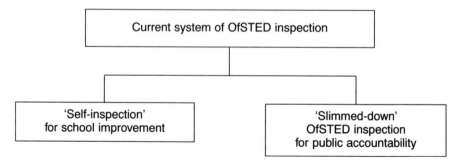

Figure 12.1 The role of self-inspection in a revised Inspection Framework – an overview

The current system of OfSTED inspection

OfSTED inspectors apply the Inspection Framework to make judgements about aspects of the school, the curriculum provided, the quality of education, leadership and the management of staff and resources. The judgements contained in the inspection report are the result of classroom observations, meetings with parents, interviews with staff and governors, study of children's work and scrutiny of documents provided by the school.

*** Replaced by two separate processes which both contribute to the outcomes of the report ***

Self-inspection for improvement

People involved in self-inspection	Frequency	Self-inspection activity
1. Head, SMT, governors, LEA officers and possibly an external consultant	Annually	Benchmarking through the identification of good practice in other schools
2. Head, SMT, governors, LEA officers and possibly an external consultant to help with the interpretation of the data	Annually	Comparative data analysis. Discussion of PANDA. Action planning
3. Teaching staff	As required	Assessment and recording of pupil progress
4. A teacher colleague, a head of dept. or co-ordinator, a senior manager or external adviser or consultant	Once each term or as necessary	Evaluation of a lesson, discussion of its strengths and weaknesses and plans to meet objectives. Links to appraisal
5. Teaching staff	As necessary	Maintain a record of information (the teaching profile) about the monitoring of teaching quality, pupil progress and action plans. Link to portfolio of CPD and threshold (Green Paper)
6. The relevant head of department or (in primary schools) the headteacher	Annually	Evaluation of the quality of teaching which draws on the information collected at 1, the data collected at 2, and 3, the reports made at 4 and the profile (see 5)
7. Governing body and SMT	Annually	Select areas for self-evaluation which relate to the school's (and occasionally national) priorities

OfSTED inspection for accountability

Inspection activity	Matter to be reported
Study teachers' self-inspection profiles and interview a small sample of the teaching staff about the action they have taken as a result of the school's monitoring and evaluation of lessons	The adequacy of individual teachers' self-inspection data, the school's findings about the quality of teaching and the thoroughness with which monitoring has been carried out. Where data are poor make recommendation for a full inspection
Study the school/LEA/governors' annual reviews of data on standards and progress and meet with the head, chair of governors and LEA representatives	Comment on the accuracy of the joint school/LEA annual reviews of standards and progress, benchmark data and the action taken as a result
Study schemes of work, IEPs, curriculum plans, pupil records and samples of pupils' work	Report on the implementation of the National Curriculum and statutory requirements and the measures needed for compliance
Study head's statement, talk to a small sample of teaching and support staff and governors. Discuss school ethos and values at parents' meeting and with pupils	Report on the effectiveness of the governors, the head and senior managers
Study relevant documents and records provided by the school	Report on staffing levels, qualifications, experience, morale, turnover, absenteeism, and on the effectiveness of staff development
Investigate pupil attainments, value-added factors, attainment of targets and budget information	Report on value for money and the use of finance and other resources Report on pupil attainment and value-added
Meet with parents and distribute questionnaire	Report the views of parents
Examine registers, headteacher's form and other school records	Report pupil truancy, attendance, exclusions and unsatisfactory behaviour

Figure 12.2 A revised inspection framework to achieve a separation of school improvement and accountability functions

aspects of the Inspection Framework in ways that could be adapted to meet the needs of individual schools. It is an activity that can be moderated by OfSTED and supported by LEAs or, if appropriate, other consultants that the school chose to employ. The centrally determined requirements ought not to be so demanding that they did not allow time for schools to select their own priorities for self-evaluation or self-inspection. Schools, with guidance from OfSTED and support from LEA advisers, should assume responsibility for the continuous monitoring of teacher performance and pupil attainment and progress. Self-inspection is thus seen as a mechanism for separating OfSTED's accountability and improvement functions and providing all 'self-inspecting' schools with some minimum entitlement to consultancy and support for development.

The reason for wanting to use a revised version of the Inspection Framework rather than any of the other self-evaluation schedules currently available, is that its familiarity and currency mean that external and internal evaluators and OfSTED inspectors would all be dealing with similar data which had been interpreted using the same criteria. This would simplify analysis and discussion, stimulate debate and make external moderation of the system relatively straightforward. As HMCI has commented, 'schools need a strategy for appraising their own performance' (OfSTED, 1998a, p.1). LEA and OfSTED support for the process, a measure of trust in teachers' professional judgements and a willingness to accept the results of schools' continuous monitoring and evaluation as a central part of a quality assurance process are small additional steps. These changes would, nevertheless, transform the system of inspection and provide it with a very different set of relationships with schools and the school improvement process.

Improving teaching quality

Teaching quality ought not to be subject to 'praise or censure from afar' and observations and assessments should be treated as if they were an aspect of staff appraisal and performance management as in most commercial enterprises and public services. It is suggested that a slimmed-down OfSTED inspection process should become unambiguously an accountability exercise reporting, as at present, on the criteria contained in the Framework. Inspectors, we suggest, should not attempt to observe teaching unless it is necessary to sample the performance of a few teachers to evaluate the school's quality assurance processes. The proposals for 'light touch' inspections have already recognised that, in 'good' schools, it is not necessary for every teacher to be observed. We need to ask whether observing several 20-minute excerpts from the lessons of the majority (or all) of the teachers in the school is ever justified. The fact that these teachers spend weeks and sometimes months of effort in planning these lessons makes the question doubly pertinent and a change would ensure that 'pre-inspection panic' and 'post-inspection blues' would no longer have such damaging effects on teacher morale and pupils' education. Inspections, furthermore, would be shorter, less expensive and much less stressful events.

OfSTED would, no doubt, be very concerned that inspectors would have no first-hand evidence about poorly performing teachers. However, if all heads and governing bodies were involved in the regular collection and discussion of information about teaching quality, they would not be tempted to wait for an inspection to bring matters to a head and would be better informed about the nature of the problems and their solution. They would need to accept responsibility for supporting, retraining or disciplining weak teachers without depending on the faint hope that exposure to an external inspection will drive them from their jobs and from the profession. There are already signs that schools would take action because during the 1998–1999 school year in England and Wales more than 3,000 teachers were formally warned that the quality of their teaching was to be investigated (*TES*, 10 September 1999).

This change would refocus attention on teachers' obligation to evaluate their own performance systematically and take part in peer monitoring and discussion of the strengths and weaknesses of their teaching. Regular monitoring by heads, senior staff and external advisers or consultants would be an essential element of the system. It would be important for teachers to maintain a record of their discussions about teaching quality and of the actions taken to bring about improvements. OfSTED's role could then include the meta-evaluation of the school's efforts to improve teaching, the scrutiny of staff members' 'self-inspection' profiles and, if necessary, the sampling of the performance of teachers in the classroom as a method of comparing standards and moderating the judgements in teachers' self-inspection profiles. The fact that external inspection required the production of these profiles and a record of action taken to improve the quality of teaching throughout the school would give a greater emphasis to the importance of sustaining efforts to improve teaching quality.

The Green Paper *Teachers Meeting the Challenge of Change* (DfEE, 1998b) aimed to provide incentives for excellence in teaching and the accompanying technical document (DfEE, 1999) provided a more detailed account of how excellence should be identified. The annex to this document lists the characteristics of good teachers that might identify them as 'advanced skills' teachers who would be able to 'pass the performance threshold', be awarded an immediate 10 per cent pay rise and gain access to higher pay scales. A system in which teachers can produce evidence from a self-inspection profile could simplify this process, reduce the need for an expensive and elaborate system of external verification and enhance its prospects of producing fair results. Could it make it possible to do away with the process altogether? Can the two be more closely linked so that proposals for teacher appraisal and teacher assessment (to pass the threshold) are built into the inspection system? At the moment there are proposals to train a cadre of external assessors and verifiers to support the implementation of the Green Paper proposals. However, the requirements of the Green Paper could, in part, be met if the changes which we are proposing to the Inspection Framework were to be implemented.

The benefits

A number of other benefits would be realised as a result of separating inspection's accountability and school improvement functions and trusting most schools to contribute to the inspection with data of their own. The four main ones are as follows:

- A slimmed-down version of inspection that is unambiguously concerned with OfSTED's function of ensuring that schools are held accountable for the expenditure of public funds ensures that inspection's incompatible accountability and development functions are explicitly separated. This would allow heads to know when the school's performance is being judged and when they are being helped to bring about improvements in the school.

- The transfer of responsibility for monitoring teaching quality from OfSTED inspectors to schools' systems of self-inspection reduces the possibility that schools will be held back by 'pre-inspection panic' whenever an inspection is anticipated and 'post-inspection blues' when the inspection has been completed.

- Self-inspection creates a system for the continuous, systematic monitoring of pupils' attainment and progress. It is a vital element in efforts to improve schools and raise standards, but OfSTED inspections have not helped as much as they might with furthering this particular aim. OfSTED's plans to develop materials and encourage schools to bolt 'self-inspection' on to their existing activities is less likely to be successful than an approach that is an integral part of the inspection system. A timetable of self-inspection requirements which gave priority to the evaluation of teaching and pupil progress and attainment would allow time for the staff to identify their own targets for inclusion.

- A requirement for schools to use consultants to advise on self-inspection arrangements, check the accuracy of evaluations of teaching quality, verify decisions taken on the requirements of the Green Paper (DfEE, 1998b) and provide support and advice for new developments is seen as important. It should clarify OfSTED's accountability, functions, provide a sharper definition of the role of the LEA and dispel the notion that the expertise of LEAs has, for historical and political reasons, been allowed to become an under-used asset.

A cautionary note

Chapter 1 began by pointing out that the influence of the OfSTED discourse and its 'colonisation' of teachers' thinking has ensured there is a sense in which 'self-inspection' is already in use in schools. Even those schools that have so far clung to their own values may yet be enticed away when other schools sign up for the new 'self-inspection' training courses which OfSTED has developed (see Chapter 1). Concerns about the increasingly influential role that OfSTED plays, about the stultifying nature of yet one more use for the Inspection Framework and for the potentially damaging effect of schemes that ask teachers to monitor and evaluate the work of colleagues are bound to be expressed. Some commentators will worry that processes of monitoring and evaluation may be weak in many schools and that monitoring will be handled badly by inexperienced staff. Most teachers might well be concerned about the implications of being asked to comment on the quality of colleagues' teaching. Others will be concerned that a national system of self-inspection would spread the influence of the OfSTED discourse, sap initiative still further and cause schools to lose touch with their own frames of reference and values. However, the system we envisage would allow teachers, in a controlled way, to claim ownership of a continuous school-based process of development, ensure that the school's priorities are included in the annual self-inspection schedule and achieve a reduction in the adverse effects of inspection.

Self-inspection, used in the way we have described, is intended to reduce the intensity of teachers' contacts with inspection teams by returning responsibility for appraisal and school development to the school. It recognises that while schools have a responsibility to parents and the community for the curriculum and standards, these are matters that can be audited effectively without unnecessary disruption to the school. Some of OfSTED's current functions can be fulfilled by processes of sampling, moderation and the verification of the schools' own 'self-inspection' processes. 'Self-inspection' should reduce the intensity of external inspection, diminish its emotional impact and allow schools to reclaim a sense of ownership of the improvement process.

Self-inspection can easily be misinterpreted, especially by those who suggest that the current system of inspection is the only alternative to unaccountable, professional control of schools. Such views should not be allowed to place the goal of making most schools into self-evaluating and self-improving institutions out of reach. Nor should they distract attention from the weaknesses of an approach to inspection that is currently strong on pressure but weak in supporting schools. Few would wish to deny the value of and need for an external perspective; the key question is how can that perspective be deployed to secure institutional improvement while reassuring the various stakeholders that schools are accountable for the quality of education that they provide.

Conclusion

The previous chapter discussed some possible reasons for OfSTED's approach to school self-evaluation. It suggested that OfSTED wants to confine the use of self-evaluation to the period between inspections. In our view, this is an inadequate way of addressing the limitations of external inspection as a catalyst for school improvement and misses an opportunity to foster the growth of self-inspection skills in schools. It is suggested that the task of bringing about improvements in schools benefits from an external perspective, but it is one that should unambiguously serve the school's needs. We argue that teaching quality ought not to be subject to 'remote management' by visiting inspectors and that observations and assessments of teacher performance in the classroom are more properly an aspect of the process of teacher appraisal and continuing professional development. This final chapter has described a school's obligation to keep its progress under frequent review and to interpret its findings in the light of appropriate comparative data. Despite some reservations, it has broadly supported OfSTED's view that the Framework can provide a useful basis for self-evaluation. 'Self-inspection', it is suggested, should include an external perspective which might be provided by consultants, LEA advisers or others. OfSTED's function of ensuring that schools are held accountable for the expenditure of the public funds they receive and for the standards and progress of their pupils in National Curriculum tests and public examinations should be fulfilled through a separate version of inspection that is unambiguously concerned with public accountability but which does not include the assessment of individual members of staff.

The success of 'self-inspection' would depend on inspection teams' acceptance of and respect for information gathered and action taken as a result of schools' internal management processes. If heads and governors are to get together regularly with LEAs and analyse educational standards and review the curriculum, if they are to devise methods for the moderation of teaching quality and choose their own priorities for self-inspection, then their efforts deserve to be recognised. That recognition should include a willingness, subject to any necessary checks and moderation processes, to treat the schools' conclusions as valid outcomes for inclusion in their inspection report. It would also include a commensurate reduction in the external inspection process which would require, in most cases, fewer inspectors for less time in school. The sole purpose of this 'slimmed-down' inspection would be to provide 'a health check' which commented on the effectiveness of the school and its significant strengths and weaknesses, its educational standards and the extent to which it provided value for money. This would allow LEA advisers and other consultants to be involved in a 'self-inspection' process in a way that was free from the threat of public censure and that was unambiguously aimed at supporting a continuous process of school self-improvement. Inspection, we have concluded, need not be conducted in a public arena in order to be effective. It must, however, be done systematically.

Self-inspection is, we suggest, a more effective route to institutional improvement because of its capacity to encourage a climate of critical reflection and continuous improvement, combat complacency and ensure that progress does not decline undetected between external inspections. Schools that can 'self-inspect' and have learned to act effectively on the results of self-inspection should, we hope, have little to fear from an OfSTED reinspection. From January 2000 the headteacher's statement, which is completed just before an inspection takes place, has included an account of the school's programme of self-evaluation. We would want to see a system of self-inspection that was not simply subjected to scrutiny but signalled to schools that they can be trusted to play a part in their own inspection and benefit from the opportunity to contribute to its findings.

References

Altrichter, H. and Specht, W. (1998) Country report: Austria, in J. Solomon (ed.) *Trends in the Evaluation of Education Systems: School Self-Evaluation and Decentralisation*, Athens: European Network of Policy Makers Conference Report.

Aris, V., Davies, J. and Johnson, P. (1998) Brookfield Special School: recovery from failure, in P. Earley (ed.) *School Improvement after Inspection?* London: Paul Chapman.

Bainbridge, P. (1999) *Effective Self-Assessment: An FEFC Good Practice Guide*, Coventry: FEFC.

Ball, S. (1997) Good school/bad school: paradox and fabrication, *British Journal of Sociology of Education*, Vol. 18, no. 3, pp.317–36.

Bernstein, B. (1970) Education cannot compensate for society, *New Society*, Vol. 387, pp.344–7.

Biott, C. and Gulson, J. (1999) Headteachers taking over failing schools: tales of good stewardship and learning at work, *Journal of In-service Education*, Vol. 25, no. 1, pp.98–108.

Borchers, P (1999) OfSTED fails to grasp subtle issues of poverty, *Times Educational Supplement*, 18 June.

Brimblecombe, N., Ormston, M. and Shaw, M. (1995) Teachers' perceptions of school inspection: a stressful experience, *Cambridge Journal of Education*, Vol. 25, no. 1, pp.53–61.

Brimblecombe, N., Ormston, M. and Shaw, M. (1996) Gender differences in teacher response to school inspection, *Educational Studies*, Vol. 22, no. 1, pp.27–40.

Brunel University Centre for the Evaluation of Public Policy and Practice and the Helix Consulting Group (1999) *The OfSTED System of School Inspection: An Independent Evaluation*, Report commissioned by the Office for Standards in Inspection (OfSTIN).

Burchill, J. (1991) *Inspecting Schools: Breaking the Monopoly*, London: Centre for Policy Studies.

Byers, S. (1997) Speech to LEA leaders, DfEE press release, October.

Camp, R. (1996) *Benchmarking: The Search for Industry Best Practices that Lead to Superior Performance*, Milwaukee: American Society for Quality Control Press.

Cassidy, S. (1999) Wealth wins top marks, *Times Educational Supplement*, 21 May.

Centre for the Study of Comprehensive Schools (1994) *Inspection: Improving Schools Together*. Broadsheet no. 44, University of Leicester: CSCS publication.

Close, D. (1998) Responding to school inspection: focusing on development, in P. Earley (ed.) *School Improvement after Inspection? School and LEA Responses*, London: Paul Chapman.

Creese, M. (1997) *Effective Governance: The Evidence from OfSTED*, Ipswich: School Management and Governance Development.

Creese, M. (1999) OfSTED on governance: a view from the bridge, *School Leadership and Management*, Vol. 19, no. 2. pp.241–52.

Creese, M. and Earley, P. (1999) *Improving Schools and Governing Bodies: Making a Difference*, London: Routledge.

Croxford, L. and Cowie, M. (1996) *The Effectiveness of Grampian Secondary Schools*. Report of a research programme undertaken by Grampian Regional Council and the Centre for Educational Sociology, Edinburgh: CES.

Cuckle, P., Hodgson, J. and Broadhead, P. (1998) Investigating the relationship between OfSTED inspections and school development planning, *School Leadership and Management*, Vol. 18, no. 2, pp.271–83.

Cullingford, C. (ed.) (1999) *The Inspector Calls*, London: Kogan Page.

Cullingford, C. and Daniels, S. (1999) The effects of inspections on school performance, in C. Cullingford (ed.) *The Inspector Calls*, London: Kogan Page.

Dalin P. (1998) *School Development Theories and Strategies*, London: Cassell.

Davis, H., Day, C., Cox, A. and Cutler, L. (forthcoming) Child and adolescent mental health needs assessment and service implications in an inner city area, *Clinical Child Psychology and Psychiatry*.

Department for Education/OfSTED (1995a) *Governing Bodies and Effective Schools*, London: Department for Education.

Department for Education/OfSTED (1995b) The improvement of failing schools: UK policy and practice 1993–1995. OECD UK Seminar, November, London: DfE.

Department for Education and Employment (1996) How weak schools recover: September 1993 to June 1996. Background note for conference at Institute of Education, London.

Department for Education and Employment (1997a) *Excellence in Schools*, London: Stationery Office.

Department for Education and Employment (1997b) *Setting Targets for Pupil Achievement: Guidance for Governors*, London: DfEE.

Department for Education and Employment (1997c) *The Road to Success: Four Case Studies of Schools Which No Longer Require Special Measures*, London: DfEE.

Department for Education and Employment (1998b) *The National Literacy Strategy*, London: The Stationery Office.

Department for Education and Employment (1998) *Teachers Meeting the Challenge of Change*, London: DfEE.

Department for Education and Employment (1999) *Teachers Meeting the Challenge of Change, Technical Document*, London: DfEE.

Department for Education and Employment/OfSTED (1999) *Helping Schools to Carry Out 'Self-Evaluation'*, London: DfEE.

Dixon, S. (1996) *Self-Assessment of Colleges*, Coventry: FEDA/FEFC.

Dunning, G. (1996) Management problems of new primary headteachers, *School Organisation*, Vol. 16, no. 1, pp.111–28.

Earley, P. (1997) External inspections, 'failing schools' and the role of governing bodies, *School Leadership and Management*, Vol. 17, no. 3, pp. 387–400.

Earley, P. (1998a) Governing bodies and school inspection: potential for empowerment? In P. Earley (ed.) *School Improvement after Inspection? School and LEA Responses*, London: Paul Chapman.

Earley, P. (ed.) (1998b) *School Improvement after Inspection? School and LEA Responses*, London: Paul Chapman.

Earley, P. (2000) Monitoring, managing or meddling? Governing bodies and the evaluation of school performance, *Educational Management and Administration*, Vol. 28, no. 2, pp.199–210.

Earley, P., Fidler, B. and Ouston, J. (1996) (eds) *Improvement Through Inspection? Complementary Approaches to School Development*, London: David Fulton.

Earley, P. and Fletcher-Campbell, F. (1992) *The Time to Manage? Department and Faculty Heads at Work*, London: Routledge.

Evans, J. and Penney, D. (1994) Whatever happened to good advice? Service and inspection after the Education Reform Act, *British Educational Research Journal*, Vol. 20, no. 5, pp.519–53.

Ferguson, N., Earley, P., Ouston, J. and Fidler, B. (1999a) *The Inspection of Primary Schools: Factors Associated with School Development*. Final Report to the Nuffield Foundation.

Ferguson, N., Earley, P., Ouston, J. and Fidler, B. (1999b) New heads, OfSTED inspections and the prospects for school improvement, *Educational Research*, Vol. 41, no. 3, pp.241–49.

Fidler, B. (1999) Benchmarking and strategy, In J. Grant (ed.) *Sharing Experiences: Value for Money in School Management*, York: Funding Agency for Schools.

Fidler, B., Russell, S. and Simkins, T. (eds) (1997) *Choices for Self-Managing Schools*, London: Paul Chapman.

Fidler, B., Earley, P., Ouston, J. and Davies, J. (1998) Teacher gradings and OfSTED inspections: help or hindrance as a management tool?, *School Leadership and Management*, Vol. 18, no. 2, pp.257–70.

Fink, D. (1999) Deadwood didn't kill itself, *Educational Management and Administration*, Vol. 27, no. 2, pp.131–41.

Fitz-Gibbon, C. (1997) OfSTED's methodology, in M. Duffy *et al.* (eds) *A Better System of Inspection?* Hexham: OfSTIN.

Freire, P. (1973) *Education: The Practice of Freedom*, London: Writers and Readers Publishing Co-operative.

Fullan, M. with Steigelbaum, S. (1991) *The New Meaning of Educational Change*, New York: Teachers' College Press, Columbia University.

Gann, N. (1997) *Improving School Governance: How Better Governors Make Better Schools*, London: Falmer Press.

Geer, B. (1968) Teaching, in B. Cosin, R. Dale, G. Esland and D. Swift (eds) (1971) *School and Society*, London: Routledge and Kegan Paul and the Open University.

Gois, E. (1998) Country report: Portugal, in J. Solomon (ed.) *Trends in the Evaluation of Education Systems: School Self-Evaluation and Decentralisation*, Athens: European Network of Policy Makers Conference Report.

Goldstein, H. and Spiegelhalter, D. (1996) League tables and their limitations: statistical issues in comparisons of institutional performance, *Journal of the Royal Statistical Society, Series A*, Vol. 159, no. 3, 385–443.

Gurr, D. (1999) *From Supervision to Quality Assurance: The Case of the State of Victoria (Australia)*, International Institute for Educational Planning.

Hall, V. and Southworth, G. (1997) Headship, *School Leadership and Management*, Vol. 17, no. 2, pp.151–70.

Hargreaves, D.H. (1995) Inspection and school improvement, *Cambridge Journal of Education*, Vol. 25, no. 1, pp.117–25.

Hopes, C. (1997) *Assessing, Evaluating and Assuring Quality in Schools in the European Union*, Brussels: European Commission.

Hopkins, D., West, M. and Ainscow, M. (1996) *Improving the Quality of Education for All*, London: David Fulton.

House, E. (1973) *School Evaluation: the Politics and the Process*, San Francisco: McCutchan.

House of Commons (1999a) *The Work of OfSTED*, Education and Employment Committee (4th Report), London: Stationery Office.

House of Commons (1999b) *The Role of the Governing Body*, Education and Employment Committee (5th Report), London: Stationery Office.

House of Commons (1999c) *Government's and OfSTED's Response to the Fourth Report from the Committee, Session 1998–99: The Work of OfSTED*, Education and Employment Committee (5th Special Report), London: Stationery Office.

Howson, J. (1999) Vacancies fall from 1998's record levels, *Times Educational Supplement*, 11 June.

Institution for School and College Governors (1996) *Inspection – a Weapon or a Tool, a Post-Mortem or a Health Check?* The Governors' Analysis, Occasional Papers No. 4. London: ISCG.

Jeffrey, B. and Woods, P. (1996) Feeling deprofessionalised: the social construction of emotions during an OfSTED inspection, *Cambridge Journal of Education*, Vol. 26, no. 3, pp.325–43.

Jeffrey, B. and Woods, P. (1998) *Testing Teachers: The Effects of School Inspections on Primary Teachers*, London: Falmer.

Kelly, F. (1996) Higher and Further Education colleges: approaches to institutional self-review, in Earley, Fidler and Ouston (eds), *op. cit.*

Kogan, M. (1999) The extent of national inspection in continental European countries: paper prepared for the Audit Commission, in Appendix 1 of Brunel University Centre for the Evaluation of Public Policy and Practice and the Helix Consulting Group, *The OfSTED System of School Inspection: An Independent Evaluation*, Report commissioned by the Office for Standards in Inspection (OfSTIN).

Law, S. and Glover, D. (1999) Does OfSTED make a difference? Inspection issues and socially deprived schools, in C. Cullingford (ed.) *The Inspector Calls*, London: Kogan Page.

Lonsdale, P. and Parsons, C. (1998) Inspection and the school improvement hoax, in P. Earley (ed.) *op. cit.*

Lowe, G. (1998) Inspection and change in the classroom: rhetoric and reality? In P. Earley (ed.) *op. cit.*

MacBeath, J. (1999) *Schools Must Speak for Themselves*, London: Routledge.

MacBeath, J., Boyd, B. and Rand, J. (1996) *Schools Speak for Themselves: The Case for School Self-Evaluation*, London: National Union of Teachers.

McMahon, A., Bolam, R., Abbot, R. and Holly, P. (1984). *Guidelines for Review and Internal Development in Schools (GRIDS). Secondary School Handbook*, York: Longman and Schools Council.

Matthews, P., Holmes, J., Vickers, P. and Corporaal, B. (1998) Aspects of the reliability and validity of school inspection judgements of teaching quality, *Educational Research and Evaluation*, Vol. 4, no. 2, pp.167–88.

Maychell, K. and Pathak, S. (1997) *Planning for Action Part 1: A Survey of Schools' Post-inspection Action Planning*, Slough: NFER.

Melia, T.P. (1995) Quality and its assurance in Further Education, *Cambridge Journal of Education*, Vol. 25, no. 1, pp.35–61.

Millett, A. and Johnson, D. (1998a) OfSTED inspection of primary mathematics: are there new insights to be gained?, *School Leadership and Management*, Vol. 18, no. 2, pp.239–55.

Millett, A. and Johnson D. (1998b) Expertise or 'baggage'? What helps inspectors to inspect primary mathematics? *British Educational Research Journal*, Vol. 24, no. 5, pp.503–18.

Mordaunt, E. (1999) Inspectorate independence: 'a fallacy that some inspectorates like to tell'. Paper presented to British Educational Research Association, University of Sussex, September.

MORI Social Research Institute (1998) *School Inspection Survey: Views of Primary Schools in England Inspected in Summer 1998*, London: OfSTED.

Mortimore, P. and Whitty, G. (1999) School improvement: a remedy for social exclusion? In A. Hayton (ed.) *Tackling Disaffection and Social Exclusion: Education Perspectives and Policies*, London: Kogan Page.

National Commission of Education (ed.) (1995) *Success Against the Odds: Effective Schools in Disadvantaged Areas*, London: Routledge.

Office of Review (1996) *Guidelines for School Self-Assessment* (draft), Melbourne, Victoria: Department of Education.

Office of Review (1997) *An Accountability Framework*, Melbourne, Victoria: Department of Education.

Office of Review (1998a) *Monitoring Staff Opinion*, Melbourne, Victoria: Department of Education.

Office of Review (1998b) *How Good is Our School? School Performance for School Councillors*, Melbourne, Victoria: Department of Education.

Office of Review (1998c) *School Review: Guidelines for Independent Verification of School Self-Assessments*, Melbourne, Victoria: Department of Education.

Office of Review (1999) *School Review 1999–2000 Conference*, Victoria, Australia: Office of Review.

Office for Standards in Education (1994/5) *The OfSTED Handbook: Guidance on the Inspection of Nursery and Primary Schools*, London: HMSO.

Office for Standards in Education (1995) *Planning Improvement: A Report on Post-Inspection Action Plans*, London: HMSO.

Office for Standards in Education (1996) *School Inspection: A Guide to the Law*, London: OFSTED.

Office for Standards in Education (1997a) *Update 24*, London: OFSTED.

Office for Standards in Education (1997b) *From Failure to Success*, London, OFSTED.

Office for Standards in Education (1998a) *School Evaluation Matters*, London: OFSTED.

Office for Standards in Education (1998b) *Making the Most of Inspection: A Guide to Inspection for Schools and Governors*, London: OFSTED.

Office for Standards in Education (1998c) *School Inspections: A Guide for Parents*, London: OFSTED.

Office for Standards in Education (1998d) *Inspection '98: Supplement to the Inspection Handbooks Containing New Requirements and Guidance*, London: OFSTED.

Office for Standards in Education (1999a) *Lessons Learned from Special Measures*, London: OFSTED.

Office for Standards in Education (1999b) *The Annual Report of Her Majesty's Chief Inspector of Schools. Standards and Quality in Education 1997/98*, London: Stationery Office.

Office for Standards in Education (1999c) *Secondary Schools Panda Annex, 1998 Data*, London: OFSTED.

Office for Standards in Education (1999d) *School Inspection: A Guide to the Law,* London: OFSTED.

Office for Standards in Education (1999e) *Inspecting Schools,* London: OFSTED.

Ouston, J. (1999) Education policy and equity in the inner cities. Keynote paper presented at the British Educational Management and Administration Society Annual Conference, Manchester, September.

Ouston, J., Earley, P. and Fidler, B. (1996) (eds) *OFSTED Inspections: the Early Experience,* London: David Fulton.

Ouston, J., Fidler, B. and Earley, P. (1998) *Making the Most of Inspection: The Impact of OFSTED Inspection on Secondary Schools,* Final Report to the Nuffield Foundation.

Ouston, J., Davies, J., Fidler, B. and Earley, P. (1998) *The Reinspection of Secondary Schools: A Different Impact the Second Time Around?* Final report to the Nuffield Foundation.

Pike, C. (1999) *Using Inspection for School Development,* Oxford: Heinemann.

Power, M. (1997) *The Audit Society,* Oxford: Oxford University Press.

Reynolds, D. (1996) Turning around the ineffective school: some evidence and some speculations, in J. Gray, D. Reynolds, C. Fitzgibbon and D. Jesson (eds) *Managing Traditions: The Future of School Effectiveness and School Improvement Research,* London: Cassell.

Riley, K. (1996) Operating with blunt instruments, *Guardian,* 26 November.

Rose, J. (1995) OFSTED inspection: who is it for? *Education Review,* Vol. 9, no. 1, pp.63–6.

Russell, S. (1996) The role of school managers in monitoring and evaluating the work of a school: inspectors' judgements and schools' responses, *School Organisation,* Vol. 16, no. 3, pp.325–40.

Salmon, J. (1997) Back from the brink, *Guardian Education,* 28 January.

Scanlon, M. (1999) *The Impact of OFSTED Inspections,* Slough: NFER.

Scanlon, M., Earley, P. and Evans, J. (1999) *Improving the Effectiveness of School Governing Bodies,* London: Department for Education and Employment.

Schagen, I. (1999) Exploring school effectiveness and 'value-added quadrants' via GCSE performance data. Unpublished NFER paper.

Sharron, H. (1996) Back from the brink: first failing school gets all-clear, *Managing Schools Today,* January, pp.12–14.

Southworth, G. and Fielding, M. (1994) School inspection for school development, in G. Southworth (ed.) *Readings in Primary School Development,* London: Falmer.

St John Brookes, C. (1997) *Schools Under Scrutiny,* Paris: OECD.

Stark, M. (1998) No slow fixes either: how failing schools in England are being restored to health, in Stoll and Myers, *op. cit.*

Stoll, L. and Myers, K. (eds) (1998) *Schools in Difficulties: No Quick Fixes,* London, Falmer.

Teacher Training Agency (1995) Combating failure at school, OECD UK Seminar, November, London: DfEE.

Webb, R., Vulliamy, G., Hakkinen, K. and Hamaleinen, S. (1998) External inspection or school self-evaluation? A comparative analysis of policy and practice in primary schools in England and Finland, *British Educational Research Journal* , Vol. 24, no. 5, pp.539–56.

Wilcox, B. and Gray, J. (1996) *Inspecting Schools: Holding Schools to Account and Helping Schools to Improve*, Buckingham: Open University Press.

Wilkinson, M. and Howarth, S. (1996) What are they looking for and how do we know?, *Education 3 to 13*, Management Issues Supplement, June, pp.32–6.

Wragg, T. (1997) Inspection and school self evaluation, in M. Duffy *et al.* (eds) *A Better System of Inspection?* Hexham: OfSTIN.

Appendix: A summary of the data sources

From 1994 to 1996 the researchers received a small grant from the British Educational Management and Administration Society which allowed them to undertake four postal surveys of secondary schools. These included all secondary schools inspected in the autumn terms of 1993 and 1994.

The Nuffield Foundation funded the research programme into school inspection from 1996 to 1999. This included three linked projects:

- secondary school inspection (1996–1998)
- reinspection (1998)
- primary school inspection (1998–1999).

The main sets of data obtained for all three research projects were similar: postal questionnaires, face-to-face interviews with headteachers, teachers and governors, telephone interviews with heads and an analysis of school documents. An outline of the sources of data is given below for each of the linked projects (see Tables 1–3).

Secondary school inspection (1994–1998)

Table 1 provides an outline of the data sources (five surveys, 15 case studies and follow-up interviews).

The 'case study' interviews took place in 15 secondary schools which had been inspected in the autumn term 1993: a total of 76 interviews were conducted – 69 teachers and seven governors. Heads were also interviewed. All these schools had responded to previous questionnaires giving information about their response to inspection, and the progress they had made in implementing the key issues for action. In addition, telephone interviews were undertaken with headteachers of 20 schools inspected in the autumn term 1994 and 20 inspected in the autumn term 1996. These 55 schools were selected to represent the range of responses to OfSTED and none were 'in special measures'. The 1993- and 1994-inspected schools were chosen on the

Table 1   The research programme – secondary schools

Date Inspected	Returned first questionnaire	Returned second questionnaire	Interview sample selected from those who answered first and second questionnaire	Nuffield Foundation funded study
Autumn 1993	Summer 1994	Summer 1995	Those within reach in one day's travel from London	Schools visited October 1996- March 1997
N=282 (1993 cohort)	N=170 (Response rate =60%)	N=87 (Response rate =51%)	Interviews with heads (N =35)	15 case studies (76 interviews)
Autumn 1994	Summer 1995	Summer 1996	20 telephone interviews with heads taken from sample of 113	Telephone interviews March–June 1997 N=20
N=399 (1994 cohort)	N = 252 (Response rate = 63%)	N = 113 (Response rate = 45%)		
Autumn term 1996	Summer 1997	No second questionnaire	20 telephone interviews with heads taken from sample of 305	Telephone interviews Summer 1997 N=20
N=383 (1996 cohort)	N=305 (Response rate =80%)			

basis of their own reported progress on implementing the inspectors' key issues for action.

The 1997 postal survey included all secondary schools inspected in the autumn term 1996. The 20 interviewed headteachers were selected according to their evaluation of how worthwhile the inspection had been for their school development: schools ranged from very positive to very negative.

Reinspection of secondary schools (1998)

Table 2   The research programme – secondary school reinspection

April 1997	10 out of 15 schools scheduled for reinspection
November 1997 to May 1998	9 of the 10 schools were reinspected by OfSTED
A month before second inspection	Questionnaires and telephone interviews with headteachers
Two to three months after second inspection	Collection of documentation on all 9 schools. Visits completed with 7 of the 9 schools

In 1997–8 ten of the secondary schools which were first inspected in the autumn term 1993 were scheduled for reinspection. These schools had already completed two questionnaires (in 1994 and 1995) about their first inspection and its consequences, and interviews had been held with staff (in 1997). One of the schools subsequently deferred its inspection due to a major building programme and was therefore excluded from this study.

Nine schools were the focus of the research on reinspection undertaken in 1998. Headteachers were interviewed before the second inspection, and heads and staff afterwards. The interviews (= 56) focused on the schools' experience of, and responses to, the second inspection, and their perceptions of the links between first and second inspection. The research investigated the extent to which the report's key issues were the focus of the second inspection and the ways in which they were approached. It has also explored how the experience of the first inspection determined the schools' preparation for their second inspection, and their responses to it.

Primary school inspection (1998–1999)

Table 3　The research programme – primary schools

Date Inspected	Returned first questionnaire	Returned second questionnaire	Interview sample selected from those who answered first and second questionnaire	Nuffield Foundation funded study, schools visited
Spring term 1997 N=500	Spring 1998 (Survey A) N=374 (Response rate =75%)	No second questionnaire	9 case studies	Summer 1998
Summer term 1998 N=500	Spring 1998 (Survey B1) N= 370 (Response rate =74%)	Autumn 1998 (Survey B2) N= 311 (Response rate =88%)	6 case studies	Autumn 1998

The primary school research project was based on the findings of national surveys of two randomly selected samples of primary heads whose schools had been inspected in the summer term 1997 or in the summer term 1998. Response rates for both groups were very high. A follow-up questionnaire survey of the second sample of heads was conducted about three to six months after their inspection had been completed, again with an excellent response rate (88%). (This was calculated after removing the six case studies and the small number who had removed their identification number.)

In addition, a random sample of over 250 registered inspectors was sent a questionnaire and about two-thirds responded (n=169).

A further source of evidence for the primary project was provided by case studies of 15 schools selected from the above two samples. Nine schools from the initial heads' sample and six schools from the second sample were selected for the case studies. As in the secondary project, all of these schools were in the south east of England, within 100 miles of London, and with the exception of some small rural schools were easy to reach by public transport. The six case study schools from the second survey were similarly carefully selected and included two inner-city, two urban/suburban and two rural schools with contrasting expectations of the inspection process.

In the case study schools from Survey A, the head, the deputy head, the co-ordinators for mathematics, English and science, and at least one governor, were interviewed using a semi-structured interview schedule. Six months later, and five terms after the inspection had taken place, the head-teachers of these nine case study schools were contacted again and arrangements were made to re-interview them by telephone. These interviews focused on progress since the case study had been completed and the heads were invited to describe recent developments in the school and the latter's relationship, if any, to the post-inspection action plan. A total of 60 interviews and nine follow-up telephone interviews were successfully conducted in these case study schools.

In the Survey B schools, interviews were held with the head, the maths and English co-ordinators and the chair of governors. Again, a semi-structured interview schedule was used. Twenty-two interviews were completed in the Survey B case studies.

The case study schools were few in number and were not intended to be a representative sample of any kind, although attempts were made to ensure that examples were included of a variety of responses to OfSTED inspection. They were undertaken primarily to collect illustrative material from a range of schools and to provide further insights into the findings of the head-teacher surveys.

Index